THE LITTLE BOOK
OF
VENTURE CAPITAL
INVESTING

Little Book Big Profits Series

In the *Little Book Big Profits* series, the brightest icons in the financial world write on topics that range from tried-and-true investment strategies to tomorrow's new trends. Each book offers a unique perspective on investing, allowing the reader to pick and choose from the very best in investment advice today.

Books in the *Little Book Big Profits* series include:

The Little Book That Still Beats the Market by Joel Greenblatt
The Little Book of Value Investing by Christopher Browne
The Little Book of Common Sense Investing by John C. Bogle
The Little Book That Makes You Rich by Louis Navellier
The Little Book That Builds Wealth by Pat Dorsey
The Little Book That Saves Your Assets by David M. Darst
The Little Book of Bull Moves by Peter D. Schiff
The Little Book of Main Street Money by Jonathan Clements
The Little Book of Safe Money by Jason Zweig
The Little Book of Behavioral Investing by James Montier
The Little Book of Big Dividends by Charles B. Carlson
The Little Book of Bulletproof Investing by Ben Stein and Phil DeMuth
The Little Book of Commodity Investing by John R. Stephenson
The Little Book of Economics by Greg Ip
The Little Book of Sideways Markets by Vitaliy N. Katsenelson
The Little Book of Currency Trading by Kathy Lien
The Little Book of Stock Market Profits by Mitch Zacks
The Little Book of Big Profits from Small Stocks by Hilary Kramer
The Little Book of Trading by Michael W. Covel
The Little Book of Alternative Investments by Ben Stein and Phil DeMuth
The Little Book of Valuation by Aswath Damodaran
The Little Book of Bull's Eye Investing by John Mauldin
The Little Book of Emerging Markets by Mark Mobius
The Little Book of Hedge Funds by Anthony Scaramucci
The Little Book of the Shrinking Dollar by Addison Wiggin
The Little Book of Market Myths by Ken Fisher and Lara Hoffmans
The Little Book of Venture Capital Investing by Louis C. Gerken with
    Wesley A. Whittaker

THE LITTLE BOOK

OF
VENTURE CAPITAL
INVESTING

*Empowering Economic Growth
and Investment Portfolios*

LOUIS C. GERKEN

with

WESLEY A. WHITTAKER

WILEY

To my daughter Alexandra,
the hardest worker I know.

Contents

Acknowledgments   ix

An Introduction to Venture
Capital Investing   xi

Chapter One
**An Historic Overview of
Venture Capitalism**   1

Chapter Two
The VC Industry Today   23

Chapter Three
The Value Proposition   45

Chapter Four
Prevailing Investment Climate   71

Chapter Five
**Field Guide for VC Investing
Options—Nonlisted** 105

Chapter Six
Investment Options—Listed 145

Chapter Seven
**Investment Process—Sourcing
and Screening** 165

Chapter Eight
**Investment Process—Due Diligence
and Selection** 179

Chapter Nine
**Investment Process—Portfolio
Construction, Monitoring,
and Monetizing** 209

Appendix: Resources 237

Notes 252

About the Authors 261

Acknowledgments

---~---

It occurred to me as I started writing this book that I wanted to draft this section and compare it with how I felt about the contents when it was completed. In a book with as many invaluable sources as *The Little Book of Venture Capital Investing*, it goes without saying that there are many people from whom I am constantly learning and who have greatly influenced my thinking and views. *Venture Capital Investing* owes a great deal to Wesley Whittaker, my talented co-writer; thank you so much to John Wiley & Sons for the referral. Thanks to editor Debra Englander and her terrific colleagues at Wiley for believing in me as a first-time author. A special thank-you also goes out to my partners and professional staff at Gerken Capital; thank you Carla, Pankti, Anthony, Valerie, Pierre, Elizabeth, Peter, Laura, and

Yaneth for the faithful support that allowed me the time to indulge in this first book-writing journey, about a business that I continue to enjoy. The industry's guardian angels have blessed me with financial success, so I can truly say that I still work as hard as I do because I was fortunate to leverage something that I am really passionate about into a career.

I also wish to give recognition to all the VC industry pioneers, current pathfinders, and tomorrow's trailblazers who never cease to amaze me with their savvy determination and survival skills. I see no limit to what is possible by America's entrepreneurs when unbridled to do what they do best.

Special thanks also goes to the wealth of sources I accessed to write this book, where there is such an abundance of industry data and intellectual capital available for a first-time author to access.

Lastly, I give special recognition to my parents who started me on the path to investing when they seeded my first investment portfolio at age 12 (Litton Industries, LTV, and PSA—sadly now all defunct enterprises).

In closing, I trust that this *Little Book* will be helpful in some small way to small business owners—who make up 93 percent of all businesses in the United States, who work tirelessly and risk so much. They deserve better access to growth capital and the opportunity to become one-percenters.

An Introduction to Venture Capital Investing

~

Occupy Wall Street protesters are planning to occupy the subway in New York City; because if there's one place to confront the nation's wealthiest 1 percent, it's the subway.

—Conan O'Brien

Who Are the 99% and Why Are They So Angry?

In September of 2012, I saw a headline on the inner pages of my *Wall Street Journal*, "Occupy Movement Turns 1 Year Old. Its Effect Still Hard to Define." Under the headline were details of arrests for disorderly conduct and photos of what looked like the aftermath of a tornado. Clues to the protestors' incongruent discontent were scattered through the crowd on professionally printed signs and hand-painted placards in fractured disarray.

The CRISIS is CAPITALISM

IPO = I'm Pissed Off

Where is the CHANGE we voted for?

I'm so angry, I made a sign

The obvious disconnect was that the protestors were actually beneficiaries of the successful ventures of the 1 percent they so willingly maligned. The entire Occupy protest was conceived, coordinated, and thoroughly documented on various forms of social media, from Tumblr to Skype to Facebook to Twitter. The protests were photographed on Apple iPhones and Android phone cameras. The protestors kept up their energy by chugging Red Bull and eating LUNA bars. They filled Zucotti Park with nylon popup tents from Ozark Trail, slept in North Face sleeping bags, kept warm with Coleman heaters while sipping Starbucks lattes. Some signs were hand-painted, but many were printed professionally at FastSigns or FedEx Office. FedEx also delivered the Guy Fawkes masks and tricorner hats that were ordered from eBay. Donations to feed and support the long-term "committed" protestors were raised through KickStarter. Corporate logos adorned hoodies, shirts, shoes, and denim jeans every-where. No matter how socially aware and progressive the 99-percenters fancied themselves, this disgruntled and unfocused multitude seemed blissfully ignorant of the fact that if it wasn't for capitalism, none of the resources they had relied on to fuel their righteous indignation would even exist. This global exercise of political democracy was only made possible by the economic democracy afforded by the brand of capitalism which has been practiced in America since the latter half of the twentieth century. As American philosopher and educator Mortimer Adler wrote in the preface of *The Capitalist Manifesto* (New York: Random House, 1958), which he co-wrote with Louis Kelso, "Democracy requires an economic system which supports the political ideas of liberty and equality for all. Men cannot exercise freedom in the political sphere when they are deprived of it in the economic system."

In other words, the Occupy protestors were right to be angry at the excesses and abuses of the elitist few, but their anger and frustration had been hijacked by those with a subversive political agenda against the only economic system that has actually improved the lives of all mankind. Fraud, deceit, and corruption in both the financial system and in the government regulatory sector are the true culprits. The crony capitalists definitely need to be brought to justice in order to restore the integrity of the real free market system; however, history has proven conclusively that socialism, communism, and anarchy are not the remedy for the excesses of criminals and evil doers.

The irony of the entire Occupy movement is that it was made possible by the very thing it decried—capitalism—and venture capitalists (VCs) in particular. Each of the companies represented by the countless logos and slogans that pervaded the Occupy protests and their multiple locales benefited, early in its conception, from an infusion of capital made by private investors who saw enormous potential and bore personal financial risk to fund the particular technology, product, or service that enabled the movement's effectiveness and the protestor's comfort. The return on that investment came about through persistent work, the maximization of available resources, the public's perception of a fair exchange of value, and YES a lot of luck. It is the true manifestation of the American Dream.

Capitalism, especially in the free market paradigm, is not the zero sum game the Occupy evangelists would have you believe. Every time people take a risk with their own money and end up winning, their good fortune does not mean that someone else lost. That is a ludicrous proposition believed only by the ill-informed or the leftist ideologue. That is the Big Lie told to fuel the envy and bigotry of the ignorant in order to promote a political and economic agenda. There is a much larger percentage of Americans who have achieved financial success than 1 percent of the population. Neither is 99 percent of the population shut out of opportunities that are still afforded to those who live in this greatest of nations. That is a propagandist distortion of statistics to the grossest extreme for purely nefarious reasons. The political paradigm put forth by the inciters behind the Occupy movement calls for sublimating the individual for the good of the collective; surrendering the inherent greed of private property rights for the altruistic enrichment of the community; and achieving a fair and equitable outcome for society by redistributing the ill-gotten gains of the successful in order to supplement the lifestyle choices of the under-achievers. Really?

The demonization of the economically successful is not at all about fairness and equality. It's about political power and economic control; the seizure of political power by those who cannot possibly gain it through reasoned public discourse and the theft of wealth that they desire but are unwilling to obtain through traditional, legitimate means. It is not fair. It is not democratic. It is unethical and it is totally antithetical to what it means to be an American.

America was built on the premise that if you have a dream, set your goals, and work hard to achieve it, you can accomplish anything. How did we become the global vortex for demonizing success? How does transforming our commercial and financial centers into landfills of consumer excess serve to bring about constructive resolution of the gulf between the have-lots and the have-nots? Whining pithy slogans based upon entitlement expectations and offering no comprehensive solutions are not synonymous with civil disobedience. We must confront the fact that the American people have allowed a few sociopathic narcissists to steal their dreams along with their money. And we must refuse to accept the hysterical, illogical, and unfounded rhetoric that it is "unfair" and "evil" for an individual to use her own vision, analysis, courage, and due diligence and to invest her own money to underwrite someone else's dream of starting a private business, creating jobs and contributing to the economic health and social well-being of the community.

What Is Venture Capital Investing?

Venture capital investing is a lot like the old baseball adage: You win some, you lose some, and some get rained out. There is no secret formula or guaranteed path to success, especially in the field of venture capital investing. Many venture capitalists have lost their entire investment when the once-brilliant ideas they funded foundered in the competitive marketplace or got torpedoed by even greater innovations.

Sand Hill Road, the legendary 3.5-mile stretch of concrete that runs east from I-280 to El Camino Real in Menlo Park, California, is the financial epicenter of Silicon Valley. It is littered with the fading memories of companies and grand ideas you've never even heard of. It is also home to many early investors in businesses who went on to become household names; calculated risks made many of them quite comfortable.

The returns on the initial investment are just the tangible rewards for being a venture capitalist. Many who live and work along this short stretch of road, which skirts the north side of Stanford University, are driven by more than money. Reid Hoffman is a perfect example; the 45-year-old partner at Greylock Partners has been in on the initiation of over 80 startups including such game-changers as PayPal and LinkedIn. He sits on the board of directors for Kiva.org and is known as the consummate connector in Silicon Valley. He genuinely cares about people and making the world a better place. As LinkedIn CEO Jeff Weiner says of Hoffman, "His true north is making a positive, lasting impact on the world in a very profound way."

Hoffman is a self-identified liberal who still drives the 2002 Acura he purchased with his share of the PayPal buyout. He probably understands the angst underscoring the Occupy complaint, but it would be an incredible stretch of credibility to paint Reid Hoffman with the scarlet "1 percent" label.

How does one become a venture capitalist? For many, like Bill Joy, it was a natural progression. Born in 1954, Bill grew up in the northern Detroit suburb of Farmington Hills, Michigan. He obtained a bachelor's degree in electrical engineering from the University of Michigan and by 1979 had completed a master's degree in computer science from the University of California, Berkeley. He also holds an honorary PhD in engineering from the University of Michigan. As a graduate student at Berkeley, Joy designed and wrote Berkeley UNIX, the first open source operating system with built-in transmission control protocols for the Internet protocol (TCP/IP), which is the basic communication backbone of the Internet. He founded Sun Microsystems in 1982 and was a key designer involved with a number of Sun technologies, including the Solaris operating system, the SPARC microprocessor architecture and several of its implementations, and the Java programming language. As an inventor, Bill is named on more than 40 patents. In February 1999, his many industry contributions were recognized in a *Fortune* magazine cover story that called him the "Edison of the Internet."

His accomplishments, the product of his keen intellect and inquisitive nature, resulted in substantial financial rewards. This prompted him to pursue interests in other areas, and in 2005 Bill Joy joined Kleiner Perkins Caufield & Byers, one of the first Sand Hill Road VC firms and the company that had provided the startup capital for Sun in 1982. Joy helped develop KPCB's strategy of funding game-changing technologies that broadly address the twin problems of climate change and sustainability. His ventures included investments in wind, solar, and thermoelectric power generation; low-cost electrical energy storage; renewable fuels and green chemicals from nonfuel sources; low-embodied-energy materials; and energy-efficient electronics. He now serves as a Partner Emeritus at the firm.

My VC journey is different from Bill Joy's and Reid Hoffman's, but I believe we share some traits in common: a strong work ethic, a willingness to invest, the strong desire to make the world a better place, and an innate ability to take a setback as a learning experience and press onward. I was 16 years old when I experienced my first business failure. It was a summertime sole proprietorship called Paul Bunyan Tree Service. Due to my lack of experience in risk assessment and due diligence, I lost all my hard-earned gains paying for damages caused by a tree coming through a client's roof. It was an expensive lesson, but business fascinated me, and I was determined to learn from my mistakes.

I earned a bachelor's degree in economics from the University of Redlands and went on to receive an MBA from the Southern Methodist University Graduate School of Business and a master's degree in international business from the American Graduate School. After finishing my university studies, I was hired by The Bank of California, where I monitored privately-held companies, and subsequently worked with a pioneering emerging markets investment manager, London-based GT Capital Management. I then self-financed a start-up called TCG, a telecom consulting engineering practice, which I sold to Pricewaterhouse-Cooper's consulting practice.

This helped set the course of my life, and later I landed a job as head of Venture Capital Investments with Wells Fargo Bank, where I serendipitously developed one of the first U.S. fund of funds with Anthony Moore, one of my current partners at Gerken Capital Associates (GCA). Some of the best ideas are born by complete accident. Sometimes the best path is the one you take alone. For example, while with Wells Fargo, I had been presented with opportunities to invest in a number of "risky," early stage companies, including Sun Microsystems and Microsoft. My investment acumen aside, the organizational guidelines that governed investments of the group at that time would not even permit me to present these opportunities to the group's Investment Committee. The unintended consequence was the creation of one of the first U.S. venture capital "fund of funds."

I did a stint at Montgomery Securities Venture Capital and was subsequently hired to become a co-GP with Prutech, the venture capital investment subsidiary of Prudential Securities, founded by another one of my current GCA partners, Hugh McClung. As one of the largest U.S. venture capital funds, Prutech was responsible for completing 50 IT and biotech sector early-stage and expansion-stage investments, and was one of the first VC funds to pioneer corporate partnering as a co-investment strategy. Eventually,

I was asked to head up Prudential Securities Technology Investment Banking Division.

I left Prudential in the late 1980s, thinking I was ready for an early retirement. After a much needed vacation in South Africa, one of my favorite destinations, the entrepreneurial bug bit once again. I founded GCA in 1989 as an alternative asset fund management firm, with particular focus on alternative assets and emerging markets. Version 1.0 of our business was to act as a seeder to "next generation" alternative asset fund managers, backing more than two dozen teams. GCA morphed circa 2000 into its present v. 2.0 business—managing and advising alternative assets (private equity, venture capital, and hedge funds), and merger and acquisitions advising. I think what differentiates our approach toward investing is that we take a very active and hands-on approach toward managing assets and, as a privately owned boutique, have the flexibility to move on investment opportunities very quickly. We are not reluctant to do the heavy lifting associated with being the lead investor. We are chameleons by nature and have adapted our investment thesis and approach to the prevailing investment climates. By way of example, our latest vintage VC fund's investment strategy is to focus on start-up and/or early-stage companies and "deal fatigued" expansion-stage companies, where our value-add is more advantageous than our investment capital.

An Overview of the Venture Capital Industry

Like Bill Joy, most venture capitalists come into the industry from another field in which they have experienced success or which holds a great deal of interest for them. There is a high tech legend that Bill Joy and futurist Ray Kurzweil were having drinks in a hotel bar one night and got into a rather protracted discussion about GNR technologies—genetics, nanotechnology, and robotics—and the possibilities of reaching a point in the future where the human race becomes one with machine. This is a favorite and recurring theme in Kurzweil's writings, but it so disturbed Joy that he developed a fund to invest in GNR for the sole reason of monitoring the progress of the sector's development. Reid Hoffman started SocialNet.com as a way for students on the Stanford campus to connect with others who shared their interests. He was about seven years ahead of the social media phenomenon, but the interest has definitely influenced his investment strategies. It led to him doing everything right when he rolled out LinkedIn several years later.

VCs don't typically use a lot of their own money. That is usually an activity reserved for what is known as an angel investor and typically involves investments of $1 million or less. Venture capitalists form a firm and start a fund, which is often designated for a specific industry sector. The fund will attract money from pension funds, endowments, foundations, and high-net-worth individuals (HNWs) and family offices who are interested in either investing in that particular sector or just looking for the higher than normal return that is the attraction and the pitfall of venture capital investing. When all goes as planned, the VC finds an entrepreneur with the next big idea, invests the fund's money for an equity position, mentors the entrepreneur's management team to the point where the new company is showing success, and then exits the investment through either an initial public offering (IPO) on the stock market or a sale of the company through a merger and acquisition by another firm. The return on the growth of the VC's equity position is then returned to the fund and paid out to the fund's investors on a prorated basis. According to statistics of the National Venture Capital Association (NVCA), 40 percent of all ventures fail to ever show a positive return, while another 40 percent may eventually break even. Everybody is chasing that elusive 20 percent that is the next LinkedIn, Google, or Facebook. Those success stories are what keep the lights on in the office buildings along Sand Hill Road and elsewhere across the country.

Venture capital activity has a significant impact on the U.S. and global economies. Venture capital is a catalyst for job creation, innovation, technology advancement, international competitiveness, and increased tax revenues. According to the 2011 Venture Impact study, produced by IHS Global

Insight, originally venture-backed companies accounted for 11.87 million jobs and over $3.1 trillion in revenue in the United States (based on 2010 data). Those totals compare to 21 percent of GDP and 11 percent of private sector employment.

So, how is the VC industry doing these days? For the fourth quarter of 2012, the NVCA issued a press release with the headline: VENTURE-BACKED EXITS ENJOYED HIGHER AVERAGE VALUES ON LOWER TOTAL VOLUMES IN 2012.

According to the release, $1.4 billion was raised from eight IPOs during the fourth quarter of 2012. This was a decline in volume from the preceding quarter, but a 23 percent increase in dollars raised. For the full year, 2012 saw 49 IPOs raise a total of $21.5 billion, driven largely by the Facebook offering. This was the strongest annual period for IPOs, by dollar value, since 2000. M&A deals were down 11 percent from 2011, with 120 disclosed value deals returning $21.5 billion for full year 2012.

As detailed in other Little Books, indexing and thoughtful asset allocation are probably a solid choice for many investors' core holdings. But for those seeking exceptional gains on a long-term investment horizon, alternative investments like private equity (including venture capital) can offer an uncorrelated—and often highly lucrative—complement to an otherwise staid investment plan.

Just like other markets, venture capital experiences periodic investment cycles. Coming off the historic dot-com boom and the Great Recession that followed, venture capital has recently taken some hits but is poised for a new run. "The lesson of the late 1990s is that venture capital can be powerful at times," said Greg Turk, director of investments for the $37 billion Teachers' Retirement System of the State of Illinois. The system is increasing its allocation to venture capital to diversify its portfolio. "If you don't have it, you might miss out if venture capital returns outperform again."

Not Your Grandfather's Venture Capital

"Hold on a second," you say. "Building tangible economic value sounds great, but aren't private equity and venture capital investments only available to highly sophisticated, ultra-wealthy individuals or institutional investors?" The answer is yes . . . and no. Historically, your grandfather's venture capital tended to be a closed club to which average investors felt they could not apply. But market competition is causing venture capital to evolve in exciting new ways, which I'll tell you about in the chapters to come.

What This Little Book Is and What It Isn't

The book is not intended as a textbook on how to raise VC or as a guide to becoming the next Google. I provide an insider's view of how VC works and how to best define VC, tying its fascinating history to its transcendent present. I offer additional background into who VC investors are, what their investment strategies are, their VC performance, and the sectors they invested in, as well as the difference geography can make. We explore the multiplier impact of VC investing, both in dollar terms and social impact. We examine the prevailing investment climate, revealing startling data on new start-up growth and challenges. Then we take a look at both the private and listed venture capital investment options available to you so that you too have the ability to become a 1 percenter!

This *Little Book* outlines a practical field guide to the VC investment process—everything from setting investment criteria to monetizing VC investments.

You will find a handy Appendix with a glossary of terms and links to a due diligence checklist and additional resources pertinent to VC investing. With this information you can properly assess the risk-reward relationship of venture capital investing. I believe you will find the insights offered pleasantly surprising.

Chapter One

An Historic Overview of Venture Capitalism

Those who cannot remember the past are condemned to repeat it.

—George Santayana

Why is an historical overview of VC important? Because history does in fact repeat itself, and a study of history allows us to frame an understanding of the present and the future. The players and the investment climate change, but the entrepreneur's innate instinct to risk capital for a return is no different today from what it was when John D. Rockefeller became America's first billionaire in 1900. When Andrew

Carnegie joined forces with his childhood friend, Henry Phipps, to form Carnegie Steel in 1892, they were driven by the same conviction to improve the status quo as are the idealistic dream chasers of the twenty-first century. It was these early trailblazers who paved the way and developed the techniques that have laid the foundation for VC as we know it today.

Arguably, historians will debate the nature of history and its usefulness. This includes using the discipline as a way of providing perspective on the problems and opportunities of the present. I believe it to be an important tool in providing a systematic account and window to the future. It is patently dishonest and irresponsible to perpetuate the popular mythology that those who created great wealth in America are to be despised and that there are no useful lessons to be learned from an objective, historical review of their contributions to the subject at hand. As John F. Kennedy said, "To state the facts frankly is not to despair the future nor indict the past. The prudent heir takes careful inventory of his legacies and gives a faithful accounting to those whom he owes an obligation of trust."[1]

In the Beginning

On Sunday, May 23, 1937, John Davison Rockefeller, Sr., died just 46 days short of his 98th birthday. He left behind what is arguably the single greatest fortune ever amassed by a single businessman. He began accumulating his wealth on September 26, 1855, when he became the 16-year-old assistant bookkeeper at Hewitt & Tuttle, a commission merchant and produce shipper in Cleveland, Ohio. Three years later, he left Hewitt and formed his own commission merchant house with his friend Maurice B. Clark, using money he had saved from his $25 monthly salary and $1,000 borrowed from his father at 10 percent interest. It was during this initial period of managing a business, struggling week to week to make weekly payroll, that he discovered his innate abilities to quickly size up an opportunity, evaluate the risk-reward, and negotiate a path forward. By December 1862, Clark & Rockefeller was a going concern, making more than $17,000 annually and occupying four contiguous warehouses on River Street.

That same year, the partners invested $4,000 of company profits with a chemist named Samuel Andrews. Andrews had developed a cost-effective method for distilling kerosene from crude oil. The partners built the Excelsior Oil Works and commercialized this process, providing a cheap and efficient means of lighting to the masses.

Rockefeller was able to buy out Clark in 1865 by borrowing funds based solely upon his business reputation. He went full-time into the oil business, building another refinery called the Standard Works. On January 10, 1870, the partnership with Andrews was dissolved and replaced by a joint-stock firm named Standard Oil Company (Ohio). Sales of stock generated $1 million in capital and Standard oil controlled 10 percent of the nation's petroleum refining business.[2]

This business model served for many years as a fairly standard template for how businesses or *ventures* were formed and financed or *capitalized*. Business founders would use their own money and whatever money they could borrow from family, friends, and anyone else who would listen to their ideas for a new or improved business. The people who invested the early money usually did so based upon the founder's ability to sell them on the capability of the idea to solve a problem or provide a much needed service for which the public would clamor. This became known as *seed capital* and was usually less than $1 million. It was risky at best and often required early investors to wait until the enterprise was a profitable, going concern before they could realize a return on their investments. If a founder came up with a very good idea, he could sometimes gain financing from an *angel investor*. These were often wealthy individuals who would invest their own money into the enterprise in exchange for either some form of convertible debt, such as a 10-year bond which could be converted into stock or cash upon maturity, or in the form of a percentage of ownership of the new company or *equity*.

As all wealthy people quickly discover, the image of Scrooge McDuck romping and rolling around in his private vault on piles of gold coins and bags of currency is only true in the make-believe world of comic books. Wealth will be depleted over time if not put to work. Taxes, inflation, expenses, and frivolous spending have caused more than a few lottery winners to end up in financial straits within a very few years. Enough stories abound about spoiled, entitled trust fund beneficiaries who completely squander their inheritances that there is an ageless proverb that says "there's but three generations from shirt sleeves to shirt sleeves." Money must be put to work by being invested, either in expanding one's own business or in someone else's venture.

The Roots of Venture Capital

Carnegie Steel Company was sold to the United States Steel Corporation in 1901 for $480 million, of which about half went to founder Andrew Carnegie. The second-largest shareholder was Carnegie's partner, Henry Phipps. In 1907, Phipps formed Bessemer Trust as a private family office to manage his fortune. Four years later, he transferred $4 million in stocks and bonds to each of his five children and Bessemer Venture Partners was launched. It is regarded as the nation's first venture capital firm. According to the company's website (www .bvp.com), they currently manage "more than $4 billion of venture capital invested in over 130 companies around the world."[3]

Laurance Rockefeller inherited his grandfather's seat on the New York Stock Exchange in 1937 and wasted no time investing his inheritance in his passion, aviation. In 1938, he provided $3.5 million for Eddie Rickenbacker to purchase Eastern Airlines and invested in the McDonnell Aircraft Corporation. The Rockefeller Brothers Fund was founded in 1940 as a philanthropic foundation, to allow Laurance and his siblings a vehicle through which to provide grants that promoted the noble ideals of democratic practice, sustainable development, and peace and security around the world. Laurance supported the fund, but saw an opportunity to provide an investment vehicle for his siblings and other wealthy individuals. In 1946, he founded Rockefeller Brothers Fund, Inc., as a limited partner investment firm. The firm was one of the first to establish the practice of pooling capital in a professionally managed fund. In 1969, the company changed its name to Venrock Associates. Venrock has been one of the most successful venture capital funds and has provided early funding for startups of such Silicon Valley giants as Intel and Apple Computer. While Venrock's primary focus could be said to be firms involved with medical technology, they have spread their investments across biofuels, vehicle technology, mobile/social/digital media, software as a service (SaaS) and enterprise, and security.[4]

The post–World War II years saw rapid growth in this new style of development capital investing. John Hay "Jock"

Whitney, another scion of nineteenth-century American wealth, spent the 1930s and the early 1940s living the archetypical high society, polo-playing playboy lifestyle, investing his $100 million trust fund in the fledgling motion picture industry. In late 1945, Jock Whitney had an epiphany. He enlisted a fraternity brother named Benno Schmidt, a tall Texan with working-class roots, to be his business partner. J.H. Whitney & Company (JHW) was founded in 1946 to finance entrepreneurs who were returning from the war with great ideas, but whose business plans were less than welcome at traditional banks. Schmidt is often credited with coining the term *venture capital* as a replacement for *development capital*, although there are earlier uses of the phrase. One of Whitney's earliest and most famous investments was in the Florida Foods Corporation, later known as Minute Maid orange juice.

Today, JHW remains privately owned by its investing professionals, and its main activity is to provide private equity capital to small and middle-market companies with strong growth prospects in a number of industries including consumer, healthcare, specialty manufacturing, and business services.[5]

The First VCs

The influence of Jock Whitney in the world of venture capital doesn't end with JHW and Minute Maid. In 1957, he recruited David Morgenthaler to serve as president and CEO of Foseco, Inc., a manufacturer of industrial chemicals in the

J.H. Whitney & Co. investment portfolio. Morgenthaler made the company a multinational success before stepping down in 1968 to go into venture capital himself. He founded Morgenthaler Ventures in Cleveland and Menlo Park. Forty-three years later, the firm is still going strong. Morgenthaler Ventures has worked with over 300 young companies, including dozens of biomedical startups. Morgenthaler also served as a founding director of the National Venture Capital Association (NVCA) from 1977 to 1979.[6]

The year 1946 also saw the launch of the American Research and Development Corporation. ARDC was the brainchild of Georges Doriot, a business professor at Harvard before the start of World War II. Upon enlistment, he was given the rank of Brigadier General in the U.S. Army and served as Deputy Director of Research at the War Department. Working in concert with U.S. Senator Ralph Flanders of Vermont and MIT president Karl Compton, Doriot developed financial vehicles that allowed private sector participation in the war effort through investments in the manufacture of weapons, equipment, and supplies. After the war, Doriot continued his partnership with Flanders and Compton in ARDC. It is often called the first actual venture capital firm because it was the first to raise funds from institutional investors: $1.8 million raised from nine institutions, including MIT, the University of Pennsylvania, and the Rice Institute. ARDC also became the first private equity firm to operate as a publicly traded closed-end fund when it collected $1.7 million in a 1966 public offering. These innovations earned Doriot the moniker of "the father of venture capital."

Doriot's best move, however, was his 1957 decision to invest $70,000 with MIT engineers Kenneth Olson and Harlan Anderson to start the Digital Equipment Corporation (DEC). Following DEC's IPO in 1968, the value of ARDC's stake had grown to $355 million. The success gave an early boost to high-tech development along Boston's Route 128 and demonstrated the viability of the venture capital investment model. And, just like at J.H. Whitney & Company, ARDC employees went on to make their own mark in the world of venture capital. Bill Elfers had been the No. 2 employee at American Research & Development. When he left ARDC in 1965 to form Greylock & Co., he decided not to follow the restrictive public funding model. Instead, he operated as a limited partnership, now the typical structure for venture firms, and raised $10 million from six limited partners. A second fund followed in 1973, and last November, what's now called Greylock Partners announced it had closed the $575 million Greylock XIII Fund.[7]

Shockley Chooses Silicon

The entire VC industry has evolved from these kinds of fraternal, sometimes internecine relationships of people being brought in to work at a firm and then deciding that they would be happier on their own. There is no better illustration of this than the story of the Traitorous Eight.

William Bradford Shockley Jr. (February 13, 1910 to August 12, 1989) was an American physicist who co-invented the transistor along with John Bardeen and Walter Houser Brattain. All three were awarded the 1956 Nobel Prize in Physics. Shockley grew up in Palo Alto and did his undergraduate studies at the California Institute of Technology (Caltech). He moved to Boston to complete his PhD at MIT and immediately started working at Bell Labs upon graduation in 1936.

Despite his brilliance, Shockley was said to be "not terribly socially adept and didn't understand what motivated people very well."[8] An example of this is the story that he left Bell Labs because the company listed Bardeen, Brattain, and Shockley in alphabetical order on the transistor's patent; he felt his name should have been listed first because of the importance of his contribution. Whatever the reason, he returned to Caltech in 1953 as a visiting professor.

Shockley had become convinced that the natural characteristics of silicon meant it would eventually replace germanium as the primary material for transistor construction. Texas Instruments had started production of silicon transistors in 1954, and Shockley thought he could improve upon their developments. Arnold Orville Beckman, founder of Beckman Instruments and one of Shockley's few friends, agreed to back Shockley's research in this area as a division of his company in Pasadena, California. Shockley's mother was in declining health at the time, and he wanted to be closer to her home in Palo Alto, so a compromise was worked out. In the summer of 1956, the Shockley Semiconductor Laboratory division of Beckman Instruments opened operations in a small building located at 391 San Antonio Road in Mountain View, California.

Shockley tried to hire some of his former workers from Bell Labs, but none of them wanted to leave the high-tech research corridor that was developing along Route 128 around Boston. Instead, he assembled a team of young scientists and engineers from the West Coast. They began researching a new method for producing a cylindrical arrangement of single-crystal silicon.[9]

The Traitorous Eight

In October 1957, eight of these young and equally talented engineers reached the end of their ability to tolerate Dr. Shockley's management style. They quit the Shockley Semiconductor Laboratory and formed Fairchild Semiconductor in Mountain View. Legend says it was Shockley who branded them as "the traitorous eight" but it was really a moniker that was applied by a newspaper reporter several years later.[10]

Fortunately, the group was helped and guided by a young financier named Arthur Rock. Rock was a forward-looking investment banker at the prestigious New York investment firm of Hayden, Stone. Rock believed technology was the future for investment and happened to know Sherman Fairchild of Fairchild Camera and Instrument (FCI) in New York. Fairchild was looking for technology companies in which to invest, and the timing was perfect.

Sherman Fairchild's father, George, was one of the original partners in the formation of the Computing Tabulating Recording Company. The company was later renamed IBM with Tom Watson as president. George Fairchild was that company's first chairman, and he and Watson owned an equal number of shares in the company. Fairchild died in 1924 with his son Sherman as the sole heir. When Watson died in 1956, his estate was divided between his wife and their four children. This left Sherman Fairchild as the biggest single owner of IBM stock. He sold some of it, which was the source of funding for the Fairchild Semiconductor start-up.

An interesting bit of trivia is that Fairchild Semiconductor was started with a $1.5 million investment by Fairchild Camera and Instrument. In return, FCI received an option to buy all of the stock that the eight held plus the stock held by Hayden, Stone for $3 million. The stock was divided by Arthur Rock so that each one of the eight got 10 percent of the stock and Hayden, Stone got the balance of 20 percent for putting the deal together. This is believed to be where the

80/20 model used in venture capital LP/GP deal structuring today originated.

It was also the first venture-funded *start-up company* in the Bay Area. The company made transistors out of silicon instead of the traditional germanium and established their facility in the Santa Clara Valley. That led to the name Silicon Valley being coined in the 1970s for all of the technology companies that were spun off of or related to Fairchild in that area.

The Traitorous Eight were Julius Blank, Victor Henry Grinich, Jean Amédée Hoerni, Eugene Kleiner, Jay T. Last, Gordon Earle Moore, Robert Norton Noyce, and C. Sheldon Roberts.

Julius Blank (June 2, 1925 to September 17, 2011) set up the machine shop and the initial assembly area at Fairchild. He was also responsible for establishing the subsequent offshore manufacturing facility in Hong Kong as sales soon outpaced the young firm's domestic capabilities. This was the precursor to the advent of offshore or *outsourced* manufacturing pioneered by VC tech companies. Blank also led the establishment of an entrepreneurial business model, which was to become the template for technology firms for the rest of the twentieth century: stock options, no job titles, and open working relationships. He left Fairchild in 1969 to become a consultant and co-founded Xicor in 1978. Xicor was subsequently acquired by Intersil Corporation in 2004 for approximately $529 million.

Victor Henry Grinich (November 26, 1924 to November 4, 2000) left Fairchild in 1968 to study computer science while teaching electrical engineering at UC Berkeley. He later taught at Stanford University as well. In 1975, he published the seminal textbook, *Introduction to Integrated Circuits*. In 1978, he was appointed CEO of Identronix, the company that pioneered radio-frequency identification (RFID) systems, used extensively in antitheft tags. In 1985, Grinich founded and became CEO of Escort Memory Systems to commercialize RFID tags for industrial applications. EMS was acquired by Datalogic four years later. In 1993, he cofounded Arkos Design, a manufacturer of emulators, which was acquired by Synopsys in 1995 for $9.3 million.[11]

Jean Amédée Hoerni (September 26, 1924 to January 12, 1997) was a silicon transistor pioneer remembered for developing the planar process for manufacturing semiconductor devices such as transistors. Along with Jay Last and Sheldon Roberts, Hoerni founded Amelco, which became Teledyne in 1961 in another Arthur Rock–funded acquisition. In 1964, he founded Union Carbide Electronics, and in 1967, he founded Intersil.[12]

Eugene "Gene" Kleiner (May 12, 1923 to November 20, 2003) was an Austrian-born American engineer and venture capitalist. In 1956, he was among the first to accept an offer from William Shockley to come to California to help form what became Shockley Semiconductor Laboratory. According to Arthur Rock, Kleiner led the eight who formed

Fairchild Semiconductor. Kleiner later invested his own money in Intel, a semiconductor firm founded in 1968 by fellow Fairchild founders Robert Noyce and Gordon Moore.

In 1972 Kleiner joined Hewlett-Packard veteran Tom Perkins to found Kleiner Perkins, the venture capital firm now headquartered on Sand Hill Road. In 1978, the company added Brook Byers and Frank J. Caufield as named partners. In full disclosure, Frank Caufield is a GCA shareholder, a close friend, and godfather to my daughter.

Kleiner Perkins was an early investor in more than 300 information technology and biotech firms, including Amazon.com, AOL, Electronic Arts, Flextronics, Genentech, Google, Hybritech, Intuit, Lotus Development, LSI Logic, Macromedia, Netscape, Quantum, Sun Microsystems, Verifone, and Tandem (which Wells Fargo Ventures had the good fortune to be a co-investor in). He retired from day-to-day responsibilities in the early 1980s.

Gene Kleiner is remembered for some of his notable observations about the venture capital industry. Although reserved, he often would make a statement that so adroitly summed up a situation that they became known as Kleiner's Laws. Some of his more notable quotes are:

"There is a time when panic is the appropriate response."

"The problem with most companies is they don't know what business they're in."

"Invest in people, not just products."

"Risk up front; out early."

The last one is considered the most strategically serious of Kleiner's Laws.

Jay T. Last (born October 18, 1929) is a physicist. He left Fairchild Semiconductor in 1961 as Head of Integrated Circuit Development. He then co-founded Amelco Corporation with Jean Hoerni and Sheldon Roberts, and served as Director of Research and Development. In 1966, Amelco was acquired by Teledyne Technologies, where Last was Vice President of Research and Development for eight years. In 1989, he founded The Archaeological Conservancy, which has preserved and protected over 150 archeological sites in 28 U.S. states. From 1982 to 2010, he was president of California-based Hillcrest Press, which publishes fine art books on the history of American painting. Last has authored or co-authored a number of art books.

It was Jay Last who best summed up why it is almost always more than a single great idea that leads to a successful enterprise. In an interview by Craig Addison of SEMI on September 15, 2007, Last pointed out how groundbreaking innovations are usually the result of the past efforts of many unsung researchers.

> . . . so much is based on past inventions and looking at what is practical to make rather than the key technical thing.

When Bo Lojek wrote his book [*History of Semiconductor Engineering*], I was asked to write a little testimonial on the back and this was a quotation that I had written for Bo for his book. "You and I agree that while the world loves a hero, semiconductor progress depended on the efforts and ideas of a large number of people and that moving forward depended on contributions going back a few decades in some cases. Also, as is the case with most inventions, a number of people with access to the same pool of common knowledge were working independently at the same time to put it all together and to make the necessary extensions to the existing technology and who realized that the time was right for society to accept the new concepts."

That says that nearly all technical progress is a group effort and always has been, and that was certainly true at Fairchild, and there were a lot of unsung heroes involved in all of these things.

With all of these things it wasn't, as I said earlier, an enormous leap forward in imagination. You sit down for a few minutes and you could visualize these things. The key question was what can we make? Every day we could come up with a dozen new great ideas of things we could do but the question was, one, could we make them? And, two, would the world buy them? So we were focused a lot more than a lot of the venture capital firms are today that think the world is going to pay them for being bright and having a bright idea. We learned quickly in those days that the world doesn't work that way.[13]

C. Sheldon Roberts (born 1926) is a semiconductor pioneer. At Fairchild, Roberts was responsible for silicon crystal production. He later joined Jean Hoerni and Jay Last to found Amelco.[14]

The last two members of the Traitorous Eight have unquestionably left their mark on the history of the human race. Dr. **Gordon E. Moore** (born January 3, 1929) is an American businessman who is known as The Chairman of Silicon Valley. He is also the author of Moore's Law, his 1965 observation that the number of transistors on integrated circuit boards (and thus, computing power) doubled every two years. His business partner, **Robert Norton Noyce** (December 12, 1927 to June 3, 1990), was nicknamed the Mayor of Silicon Valley.

In July 1968, these two men left Fairchild and co-founded NM Electronics with funding again provided under the auspices of Arthur Rock, who had joined Tommy Davis in 1961 to form Davis & Rock LP. A year later, NM Electronics changed its name to Intel Corporation.[15]

Noyce is credited (along with Jack Kilby) with the invention of the integrated circuit or microchip, which fueled the personal computer revolution and gave Silicon Valley its name. The relaxed culture that Noyce brought to Intel was a carry-over from his style at Fairchild Semiconductor. He treated employees as family, rewarding and encouraging teamwork. His follow-your-bliss management style set the tone for many Silicon Valley success stories.[16]

Why Was the Venture Capital Method of Investing Chosen?

Capital for venture capital funds comes from a variety of sources. The economic boom that followed World War II saw developmental funding shift from the traditional purview of wealthy individuals and their family funds to more accessible venture capital and private equity firms. By establishing a fund that is aimed at a particular sector, venture capital firms provide a vehicle whereby qualified and institutional investors could put their money into enterprises that best represent their aims and goals.

By providing experienced management with respect to the establishment of specific funding criteria, diligently screening funding candidates, and the imposition of a professional management overlay, investors were assured that their money wasn't being wasted or squandered. More importantly, clear exit strategies were developed, and new ventures were guided toward liquidity events such as an initial public offering (IPO) or sale of the company through a merger with another firm or acquisition by a firm in a related field (M&A).

The general partners (GPs, or the investment managers of the VC funds) at the "early stage" venture capital firm would aim for these liquidity events to occur within three to seven years after initial funding in order to allow the new enterprise to mature into a profitable business. Many firms have overlapping funds set up so that there is a continuous flow of diverse funding opportunities. In either case, the goal was for the VC fund to realize a return on investment (ROI) sufficient to allow the investor participants or limited partners (LPs) of the fund to (hopefully) realize a gain on their investment.

The technology and innovations that came to market in the 1960s and 1970s saw an entirely different breed of successful inventor or researcher turned wealthy investor. In the 1980s, computing became personal, phones became cellular, and words like "apple" and "windows" took on entirely new meanings. The 1990s brought us the World Wide Web, HTML, the Pentium processor, the smart pill, and Viagra.

This past decade saw the AbioCor artificial heart representing groundbreaking miniaturization of medical technology and an artificial liver invented by Dr. Kenneth Matsumura. The Braille Glove, wearable nanotechnology, translucent concrete, and a plethora of social media platforms, applications, and computer peripherals have appeared. All of them have required someone to believe in them enough to risk putting their money where their heart is.

Just when you thought you had seen it all, a new generation comes along and offers a fresh perspective or a radical new take on what we commonly refer to today as *disruptive technology*, another VC-coined term. The world is reinvented and recreated on a constant and ongoing basis thanks to venture capital. VC investors are anything but greedy and unfeeling; quite the opposite. They are visionaries. They are the guarantors of the future. And as many as there are and as varied as their investments are, there is always room for one more person who has the ability to see dreams and the patience to help them come true.

Past Is Prologue

We opened this chapter by asserting that it is important to understand venture capital's long and storied past as a prerequisite for understanding today's climate and having insight into the future. I am hopeful that the historic anecdotes provided here give valuable insights that will help you appreciate that VC and its success are very much about people. There is no prescribed set of formulas adhering to an Austrian economics guidebook. There is no secret sauce. Time and time again, success has come down to one person getting to know the person across the table and developing the feeling that this was a person he could trust and someone he could invest in. And, as we have seen, history does often repeat itself, especially in the world of VC!

Chapter Two

The VC Industry Today

We don't care what stage a company is when we invest. In the last couple of years, the smallest we invested was $25,000 and the largest was $40 million, ranging from an idea on a napkin to a business that is already up and running.

—Jeremy Levine, Partner
at Bessemer Venture Partners

ONE GRAND SLAM HOME RUN does not make you a Hall of Fame baseball player. When searching for a VC role model or mentor, it is more important to remember that it is easy to become impressed with those one-hit wonders who, whether by good timing or good luck, have had a "100+X bagger" or investment success. One big score is an historical event, but it is, in many cases, unrelated to the skill set required for long-term success in venture capital investing. That is an achievement marked by the repeatability of the successful exit in the prevailing and constantly changing investment climates. We should instead seek out the serial repeat players: those rare gems who are not just investing a fund's money, but who also infuse the deal with their own intellectual capital, experience, and hard work. We want to find those power players who seem to have developed a sixth sense about achieving success.

Whether one is investing in a VC fund run by partners or making a direct investment run by a CEO, the key is not to be impressed with a single success or the power of their "branding." The maxim "You are only as good as your last victory" is less applicable in the VC universe than "What have you done for me lately?" Complicating this task, is that once the list of successful VC investors has been pared down to the serial winners, the list is further narrowed by the natural human tendency for the successful to enjoy the fruits of their labor and either retire or become much less active in the funds they manage or companies they run. Once a person has achieved true financial freedom, it is hard to ignore the allure of travel, leisure sports, creative arts, or philanthropy.

Adventures in VC Investing

Much has changed in the venture capital industry since those early days of Fairchild Semiconductor. Bob Noyce and Gordon Moore left Fairchild in 1968 to form Intel, and Eugene Kleiner invested in their new venture. Four years later, Kleiner would leave engineering for good and team with HP executive Tom Perkins to found Kleiner Perkins, one of the seminal venture capital firms on Sand Hill Road. These men were able to do this because Fairchild Semiconductor had been a wildly successful company and their 10 percent ownership stakes had made them wealthy men.

Their technology changed the world of electronics; however, no matter how great or needed the product may be, nothing happens until somebody sells something. In the case of Fairchild, that somebody was a non-engineer named Donald T. Valentine. He was a senior sales and marketing executive with Fairchild Semiconductor who happened to have connections with the military and convinced them to use Fairchild semiconductors in their Minuteman missile program.

Don left Fairchild to go to National Semiconductor, but kept in touch with his former colleagues at Intel. In 1972, convinced that the path to future riches was in semiconductors, systems, and software, Don founded Sequoia Capital. He was one of the original investors in Apple Computer (AAPL), Atari, Cisco Systems (CSCO), LSI Logic (LSI),

Oracle (ORCL), and Electronic Arts (ERTS). According to Don, success in today's venture capital world is reducible to a few words; dealing with change.

> You have to be interested in managing change, and you have to recognize that change is necessary. Today's solution is wrong for tomorrow. Technology changes rapidly, so you're able to see it very quickly. The evolution of handheld computers happened in three years, and you have unbelievably good products right now that were not conceivable four years ago. That's what I mean about embracing change. You have to recognize that what you have now is not the end; it's not the limit. When you can't do that change from the Walkman to the iPod, you become like General Motors. You cannot develop anything new. General Motors, in a very short period of time, lost their role to a Japanese company by the name of Toyota, who did embrace change.[1]

After having established the intellectual property (IP) while conducting our due diligence, one of the first questions we always ask our prospective portfolio companies is "What is the ongoing product development plan regarding future enhancements, such as version 2.0, version 3.0, and so on?"

Steve Blank is a consulting associate professor at Stanford University and a lecturer and serial entrepreneur. He has a blog that is widely read and has published several books on starting a successful enterprise. In a recent cover story for the *Harvard Business Review*, Blank discussed some of the changes taking place in the venture capital industry.

> Another important trend is the decentralization of access to financing. Venture capital used to be a tight club of formal firms clustered near Silicon Valley, Boston, and New York. In today's entrepreneurial ecosystem, new super angel funds, smaller than the traditional hundred-million-dollar-sized VC fund, can make early-stage investments. Worldwide, hundreds of accelerators, like Y Combinator and TechStars, have begun to formalize seed investments. And crowdsourcing sites like Kickstarter provide another, more democratic method of financing start-ups.[2]

These Angel, Accelerator, and Micro VC Funds, including our own GCA Catalyst Fund, are able to make the less than $1 million seed, start-up, or early-stage investments that the larger institutional VC funds cannot make due to their sheer size. Recognizing how underserved the sector is, GCA Catalyst is also completing diligence on a "crowdfunding" entity to take advantage of the popularity of this funding method once the 2012 JOBS Act is fully enacted.

How It All Began

Several major VC firms were started in the late 1960s to early 1970s period. Most were related to the rapid growth of technology being seen along the Route 128 corridor outside of Boston and Silicon Valley. Boston firms included Greylock Partners, founded in 1965, and Charles River Ventures (1970). The Silicon Valley area south of San Francisco Bay spawned several firms in that period which are still active, many of them located on Sand Hill Road in Menlo Park. These include Sutter Hill Ventures (1964), Morgenthaler Ventures (1968), Mayfield Fund (1969), Kleiner Perkins Caufield & Byers (1972), Sequoia Capital (1972), and Sofinnova Ventures (1974). Greylock Partners moved their headquarters to Menlo Park in 2010, but still have an office in the Boston area.

Like every other business, venture capital investing is subject to the ebb and flow of economic conditions. We created our first fund of funds in the early 1980s. Across the industry, 650 VC firms vied for a portion of the $31 billion venture capital pool that had flowed into the industry. By the end of the decade, the number of players and the size of the pool had reduced significantly.[3] The industry returned and peaked in the first quarter of 2000 with more than $28.4 billion invested across 2,160 deals. The latest statistics for Q1 of 2013, shows that 319 firms invested an average of just under $7 million across 863 transactions.[4]

The trend is coming back down with respect to the number of VC firms and the quantity and value of their investments. More than ever before, it is imperative that today's venture capitalist stay abreast of what the competition is doing. For some VCs, it is a matter of trying to determine where the trend is heading. If several firms are jumping on solar panel developers, that may indicate that someone either has or is about to make a technological breakthrough. For the contrarian, it might indicate that it is time to look for an edge in clean coal technology or more efficient steam turbines. Either way, one of the best trend references is the MoneyTree Report.

The MoneyTree Report

The MoneyTree Report (www.pwcmoneytree.com) is published on a quarterly basis by global business consultant PricewaterhouseCoopers in cooperation with the National Venture Capital Association. This report has become one of the basic VC reference sources for the financial community. Its purpose is to measure and report on venture capital investment activity across the United States, and it contains detailed quarterly results and aggregate trend data beginning with 1995 on up to the most recent quarter. The global business news organization Thomson Reuters compiles data on emerging companies that receive financing and the venture capital firms that provide it. This data are compiled and organized based upon several different criteria by PricewaterhouseCoopers, who produce and maintain the online report.

Geographical Definitions

For the most part, geography matters to VCs. They want to fund businesses located in ecosystems with the requisite VC infrastructure in place to easily access and enable success, whether it be a pool of talented engineers to recruit, serial entrepreneurs to tap into, board member talent, other VCs to co-invest with, or the abundance of support professional service providers such as IP law firms, legal and audit. Many quite frankly just prefer the flexibility to jump in the car and easily meet with their companies.

The MoneyTree Report divides the United States into 18 different regions. In the report for the first quarter of 2013, 863 deals were financed, with the average size of the financing package being about $6.8 million. The total invested in this period across the entire nation for this quarter was more than $5.8 billion. Of that total, nearly 38 percent went to fund 274 companies in the Silicon Valley region. This region is defined as northern California, the San Francisco Bay area, and the northern half of the California coastline. The New England region, which includes Maine, New Hampshire, Vermont, Massachusetts, Rhode Island,

and parts of Connecticut (excluding Fairfield County), came in second for the quarter with $677 million funding 88 projects. With 98 projects sharing $576 million, the New York Metro region, defined as the Metropolitan New York area, northern New Jersey, and Fairfield County in Connecticut, came in third with 9.83 percent. Texas had only 31 projects, but the $534 million in funding accounted for 9.10 percent of the 1Q total.

The LA/Orange County region, which includes all of Southern California (except the San Diego Metropolitan area), the Central Coast, and the San Joaquin Valley, came in fifth place with 55 projects sharing $365 million in funding. Sixth place went to the Southeast region with 33 projects spread across the states of Alabama, Florida, Georgia, Mississippi, Tennessee, South Carolina, and North Carolina. The DC/Metroplex, defined as Washington, D.C., Virginia, West Virginia, and Maryland saw 30 projects sharing about 5 percent of the total funding and was followed in eighth place by the San Diego region with 3 percent over 26 projects.

The remaining 12 percent of funding was spread over 228 projects in the following nine regions:

1. Northwest—defined as Washington, Oregon, Idaho, Montana, and Wyoming
2. Philadelphia Metro—defined as Eastern Pennsylvania, southern New Jersey, and Delaware

3. Midwest—defined as Illinois, Missouri, Indiana, Kentucky, Ohio, Michigan, and western Pennsylvania

4. Southwest—defined as Utah, Arizona, New Mexico, and Nevada

5. Colorado

6. North Central—defined as Minnesota, Iowa, Wisconsin, North Dakota, South Dakota, and Nebraska

7. Upstate New York—defined as northern New York state outside of the Metropolitan New York City area

8. South Central—defined as Kansas, Oklahoma, Arkansas, and Louisiana

9. Sacramento / Northern California / Northeastern California

There were no funding reports from the final geographic classification region, which is the combination of the outlying regions of Alaska, Hawaii, and Puerto Rico.

Industry Classifications

Just as in geography, industry classifications matters, too. The VC wants to easily access the deal flow and intellectual capital pools of talent available that address his own sector expertise, be it a university, innovation center, research hub, or corporate R&D. Being close and having easy access to this sector expertise is a great value-add to a VC.

Venture capital investing has grown to cover much more than software and semiconductors. Users of the MoneyTree

Report can monitor funding across 17 different industry classifications. The first of these is biotechnology. This industry includes firms that are developing technologies related to drug and pharmaceutical development, disease treatment, and a deeper understanding of living organisms. This industry includes human, animal, and industrial biotechnology products, services, and related hard goods like biosensors and biotechnology equipment.

Business products and services firms offer a product or service targeted at another business such as advertising, consulting, and engineering services. This category can also include distributors, importers, and wholesalers.

The computers and peripherals industry includes manufacturers and distributors of PCs, mainframes, servers, PDAs, printers, storage devices, monitors, and memory cards. It also includes innovators in digital imaging and graphics services and equipment such as scanning hardware, graphics video cards, and plotters. Integrated turnkey systems and solutions are also included in this category.

Consumer products and services industry members offer products or services targeted at consumers such as restaurants, dry cleaners, automotive service centers, clothing, toiletries, and housewares.

Electronics/instrumentation is a broad classification that covers business and consumer electronic devices such as photocopiers, calculators, and alarm systems. It also includes electronic parts and equipment, specialized instrumentation, scientific instruments, lasers, power supplies, electronic testing products, and display panels.

Financial services is an industry classification for providers of financial services to other businesses or individuals, including banking, real estate, brokerage services, and financial planning.

Healthcare services covers both in-patient and out-patient facilities as well as health insurers. Hospitals, clinics, nursing facilities, managed care organizations, physician practice management companies, child care, and emergency care are examples of fundable projects in this industry.

Industrial/energy is the category that contains producers and suppliers of energy, chemicals, related materials, industrial automation companies, and oil and gas exploration companies. Also included are environmental, agricultural, transportation, manufacturing, construction, and utility-related products and services.

IT services include providers of computer and Internet-related services to businesses and consumers, including computer repair, software consulting, computer training, machine leasing/rental, disaster recovery, web design, data input and processing, Internet security, e-commerce services, web hosting, and systems engineering.

Media and entertainment funding goes to creators of products or providers of services designed to inform or entertain consumers including movies, music, consumer electronics, sports facilities and events, and recreational products or services. Online providers of consumer content are also included in this category.

Those who manufacture or market medical instruments and devices including medical diagnostic equipment, medical therapeutic devices, and other health-related products come under the classification of medical devices and equipment.

Providers of data communication and fiber optics products and services fall into the networking and equipment classification. This includes providers of WANs, LANs, switches, hubs, routers, couplers, and network management products, components, and systems.

Retailing/distribution funding covers firms making consumer goods and services available for consumer purchase including discount stores, super centers, drug stores, clothing and accessories retailers, computer stores, and book stores. Also included in this group are e-commerce companies who sell their products or services via the Internet.

There are, of course, still funding requirements for new and exciting developments in the original venture capital classification of semiconductors. This industry classification typically includes those who design, develop, or manufacture semiconductor chips, microprocessors, or related components including diodes and transistors. It also includes companies that test or package integrated circuits.

Software is a major funding category, which covers producers of software applications for business or consumer use. This includes either bundled or unbundled software created for systems, graphics, communications and networking, security, inventory, home use, educational, entertainment, specific industries, or recreational applications.

Companies focused on the transmission of voice and data including long-distance providers, local exchange carriers, and wireless communications services and components are funded under the telecommunications classification. Also included are satellite and microwave communications services and equipment.

The final classification criterion is "other." The category includes those unique or different products or services that are not appropriately or accurately described by the other classifications.

Sector Definitions

The MoneyTree Report uses three sector classifications, which can cross traditional industry classifications. The first of these sectors is clean technology. This sector is for companies that focus on alternative energy; pollution reduction; pollution remediation; or recycling, battery technology, and power supplies and conservation. The second sector is specifically for Internet-specific ventures. This discrete classification is assigned to a company whose business model is fundamentally dependent on the Internet, regardless of the company's primary industry category. The final sector is life sciences. The life sciences sector focuses on all deals involving biotechnology and medical device companies.

Cooking the Soup

There are many other websites, like CB Insights (www .cbinsights.com) and StrategyEye Cleantech (www.strategy eyecleantech.com), who provide the serious venture capital investor with all of the data about the deals that have been made. There are even private services costing thousands of dollars that try and pick winners even before they formally pitch their ideas. The trick is finding the golden needle in the haystack. There doesn't appear to be a secret formula for picking winners ahead of the fact, but there are firms who seem to have built pretty good track records. There are also a few VCs who have established themselves as somewhat prescient. We will discuss the process for arriving at the decision about who to fund and why, but let's take a quick tour of who is doing what today.

Outstanding Venture Capital Firms

AlwaysOn (http://aonetwork.com) describes itself as "the leading business media brand connecting and informing the entrepreneurial community in the Global Silicon Valley."[5] The editors of AlwaysOn, in concert with New York–based

451 Research and the Investment Research group of Morgan Stanley, compiled the data for the total number and dollar amounts of successful M&A and IPO exits that the top 300 VC firms completed between October 1, 2010, through September 30, 2012. From this data, they determined the Top 10 VC Firms of 2012 and announced the winners at the 2012 Silicon Valley Venture Summit, held December 10th through the 12th, 2012, at The Ritz-Carlton luxury resort overlooking the Pacific at Half Moon Bay, a perennial favorite venue for VC fund annual meetings.

The analysts at AlwaysOn were not privy to the valuations paid by investors at each respective round of financing, so their list is admittedly a best educated estimation; however, the 2012 list nears an astounding $350 billion in exit value, proving that the strength of the venture-backed entrepreneurial community remains undiminished.[6] To put some context on that number and to illustrate the multiplier effect of venture capital in the economy, Microsoft paid a $33 billion dividend to its shareholders in December 2004. It was the largest payout of its time and made up 6 percent of the total increase in personal income in America for that year.[7]

The first-place firm selected for this honor was Accel Partners (www.accel.com), who were chosen not solely on the estimated $53.938 billion in exit value, but also on the strength of the underlying portfolio. These included the mobile advertising platform Amobee, which was acquired by Singapore Telecommunications; Brightcove, a global provider of cloud content services; Facebook, the ubiquitous online social networking service of which Accel still holds 10 percent equity; the electronic commerce and couponing website, Groupon; Kosmix, the Internet advertising platform, which was acquired by Walmart; NextG Networks, the consumer electronics developer, which was acquired by Crown Castle for a reported $1 billion; and Trulia, the online residential real estate platform. The Palo Alto firm was founded in 1983 by Arthur Patterson and Jim Swartz and currently manages nearly $12 billion in funds.

Second place went to venerable Greylock Partners (www.greylock.com). The 48-year-old Waltham transplant manages nearly $2 billion. Their 2011–2012 exits were worth an estimated $67.2 billion and included some familiar names such as Instagram, the online photo sharing application, which was acquired in April 2012 by Facebook for $1.01 billion. Greylock was also involved in the Facebook exit as well as the $9.31 billion IPO of professional networking site, LinkedIn. Also included were hardware firewall experts Palo Alto Networks, SaaS HR and payroll solution Workday, and online gaming platform Zynga.

Andreessen Horowitz (www.a16z.com) came in third with $60.3 billion in exit valuations. It is a $2.5 billion venture capital firm that was launched on July 6, 2009, by Marc

Andreesen and Ben Horowitz. Its 2011–2012 exits of note were Instagram, Facebook, and Skype, the voice and video conferencing application that was acquired by Microsoft in May, 2011, for $8.5 billion.

All of the Top 10 VC firms honored at this gala have offices in the Silicon Valley area, and many people believe that that is the only place where one will find the serious venture capitalists. That simply isn't true. There are many active and dynamic venture capital firms located around the country.

Harbert Venture Partners (www.harbert.net/) of Birmingham, Alabama, has over $200 million in committed capital and recently exited Agility Healthcare Solutions in a 2008 acquisition by GE.

Highway 12 Ventures (www.highway12ventures.com) is in Boise, Idaho. The VC firm was co-founded in 2000 by Mark Solon after he left Atlantic Capital Group in Boston. Highway 12 focuses on startups based in the Rocky Mountain region. Solon and company recently celebrated the exit of travel blog platform Everlater, which was acquired by AOL for incorporation into MapQuest.

In the Great Lakes region, Arboretum Ventures (www.arboretumvc.com) is a venture capital firm specializing in the healthcare sector. They invest throughout the United States, but place special emphasis on startups in the Midwest. Jan Garfinkle spent 20 years in senior management positions with bioengineering and medical device companies before she founded Arboretum in 2002. The firm is headquartered in Ann Arbor, Michigan, and currently manages approximately $235 million in capital.

Sadly, while our firm did not make the list of top 10 VC funds in generating absolute dollar IPO/M&A realizations, I am proud to share that we have been a serial investor in the VC space since 1981 and deserve an honorable mention for longevity. Gerken Capital Associates (www.gerkencapital .com) is located in Mill Valley, California, which is, figuratively speaking, light years away from Silicon Valley. We are a Registered Investment Advisor, and our asset management business is dedicated to alternative investments, with a core focus on leading—yes, doing the heavy lifting—early-stage/inflection point investments for both private and micro-cap listed companies. Our alternative investment products include both dedicated funds and separately managed accounts, aka customized accounts. Since our formation in 1989, we have been fortunate to participate in and generate top-quartile investment returns for our investors. Maybe we'll make the next AlwaysOn top 10 list!

If It Was Easy . . .

Benno C. Schmidt, Jr., is the son of the co-founder of seminal venture capital firm J.H. Whitney & Co. and an accomplished man in his own right. He is the former president of

Yale University and the former dean of Columbia Law School. In 2012, while serving as interim president and CEO of the prestigious Ewing Marion Kauffman Foundation, he oversaw a general review of the state of the venture capital industry as a whole. This review was conducted by Kauffman Quantitative Director, Bill Weeks. The foundation oversees an endowment of $1.89 billion, of which $249 million is invested in various VC funds. These are brand name funds; however, because of confidentiality provisions signed at the time of investment, neither their names nor detailed information about the funds' performance or structure can be divulged.[8] The report was targeted to an audience of institutional investors and their investment committees and trustees. It was conclusive that the traditional model of venture capital investing, which had been developed by the larger, well known firms, was not performing up to expectations. The great problem was that too many limited partners (LPs) invest too much capital in underperforming VC funds on misaligned terms.[9]

Methods and assumptions that worked in the three decades prior to the mid-1990s are no longer effective or necessarily applicable. This is borne out by a *Wall Street Journal* article that appeared in the Small Business news on September 19, 2012. The article, written by Deborah Gage, looked at research by Harvard Business School's Shikhar Ghosh. He found that if one were to change the definition of failure from the industry standard to an investor-relevant definition, the results would be dramatically and significantly altered. Industry associations like the National Venture Capital Association like to say that only about 30 percent to 40 percent of startups have a high potential of failure; meaning the company has to liquidate all assets, with investors losing all of their money.

Ghosh asserts that if the definition of failure were changed to the startup failing to see the projected return on investment, whether that means achieving a specific revenue growth rate or hitting a milestone date to break even on cash flow, the failure rate would climb to more than 95 percent of startups on an annual basis.[10]

My intention with this chapter is to better educate and build the knowledge base that VC-sector investors need in order to spot the next generation of successful VC funds and investment opportunities. Only by understanding the inner workings of the process and the motivations of the participants at every level can investors realize the returns on investment and the inner sense of positive contribution that can only come from venture capital investing.

Chapter Three

The Value Proposition

Venture capitalists are patient, long-term investors who are willing to take entrepreneurial risks alongside company founders. No other asset class has the wherewithal or the appetite for this type of critical high-risk investment in our country's most promising ideas.

—Mark Heesen, the longtime president of the
National Venture Capital Association (NVCA)

The Multiplier Effect of Venture Capital

Sometimes you get lucky, and the returns you get are not just measured in dollars and cents! In 1983, I was one of the general partners at Prutech, the Prudential Securities VC Fund

Unit. We made a seed investment in Summit Technology Inc., based in Waltham, Massachusetts. Our $3 million bought roughly 60 percent of the company. Dr. Dave Muller was the founder and CEO. He had patented the excimer laser technology while at Cornell University. Subsequently, Summit was the first enterprise to receive FDA approval to use an excimer laser for photo-refractive keratectomy and the first company to receive FDA approval to mass manufacture and distribute excimer lasers. VISX and other companies followed suit starting in 1986. The technology initially had two applications, one for laser ablation angioplasty, which Massachusetts-based Boston Scientific was to market, and the other for ophthalmic surgery; what has come to be known today as LASIK eye surgery.

In 2000, Summit Technology was sold to Alcon for $948 million. Muller went on to form other companies, including Avedro, recognized as a global leader in the development of advanced technologies for ophthalmic applications. It was impossible to calculate in the early 1980s that Summit would eventually be acquired at such an eye-popping valuation! It did so for the simple reason that Dave Muller saw a need and filled it. He developed the forerunner technology for the multitude of LASIK treatments that would dramatically improve the living standards for millions of people burdened with myopia and astigmatisms and dependent on eye glasses and contacts, including me!

Water, Water Everywhere

Yes! Money is the yardstick that we are measured by in the financial markets; however, whether intended or a serendipitous by-product, the enormous social benefits and improved standards of living are the lasting rewards which cannot be truly quantified. It is ubiquitously referred to in the industry as "social impact" investing and these opportunities are everywhere. In 2007, my co-author, Wes Whittaker, joined a fledgling angel investor firm as a project developer. His job was to travel around the country and hold "pitch sessions," at which entrepreneurs would come and present their ideas in hopes of obtaining seed capital. Although he had to suffer through some fairly unrealistic and poorly executed PowerPoint presentations, the majority of the ideas were very good. Some of them were extraordinary examples of an outside the box approach to challenges facing the global community.

One company had developed a method for causing cancer cells to virtually commit suicide. Another researcher had used a modification of analog signal processing to develop a method for warning of impending cardiac incidents. A group made a presentation featuring a variety of wind-powered generators ranging from backpack size all the way up to an integral part of a high rise apartment building. Another inventor had an idea for harnessing the wave action of the ocean to produce electrical power. An architect from Sedona was seeking funding for a fully sustainable residential community that utilized solar power, greywater systems, and a synchronous fiber optic network, which allowed the house to monitor itself and was interactive with the community. Another developer was seeking funding for an eco-resort in Costa Rica, which would provide comfortable lodging for tourists while having a minimal footprint on the rain forest in which it was to be built.

Then there were the water projects. Chlorine dioxide has long been known to be exponentially more effective for treating water and eliminating pathogens and mineral contaminants than the sodium hypochlorite, or simple chlorine, in common use today. The problem was that the generation of chlorine dioxide produced a very volatile gas that had a tendency to spontaneously explode. Consequently, generation plants were very expensive to build and maintain. Most municipalities had opted for the cheaper chlorine, despite the undesirable aesthetic drawbacks of taste and odor. A California-based company had developed a method for producing an efficacious dry powder method form of chlorine dioxide that was not only safe, but economically competitive.

Another firm from Atlanta had developed a mobile water treatment plant which fit into a standard shipping container and could be modularized. Their goal was to provide potable drinking water to areas where the water supply was no longer safe, such as those affected by environmental disasters like drought or hurricanes. Wes had an epiphany. By merging the two companies, he saw an opportunity to develop a product that would have a lasting, global benefit: mobile, plug-and-play water treatment systems.

It is these moments of synchronicity which not only drive, but also inspire most venture capital investors. It is great to make a lot of money, but as many have discovered, that is a short-lived and hollow accomplishment by itself. We are social beings at our core and we all have the need to bring value to our community in some way. Recent history has shown us that the race to accumulate earnings solely for the sake of building personal wealth ultimately leads to personal and professional dissatisfaction. There has to be more to our lives than the bottom line.

Economy and Jobs Impact

Venture capital is the DNA upon which our very successful capitalistic economy is based. To paraphrase a currently popular euphemism, VCs "built this!" Entrepreneurs and small- to mid-size enterprises, frequently referred to as SMEs, represent the overwhelming majority of U.S. businesses and employers, accounting for as much as 93 percent of all businesses in the United States. These are companies with fewer than 50 employees for small companies and up to 250 for medium-sized companies. Congressman Eric Cantor, the House Majority

Leader from the 7th District of Virginia, released a statement in November 2011 in support of Small Business Saturday, a national initiative to encourage people across the country to support their local, independently-owned businesses.

"Small businesses are the driving force of the economy and create 70 percent of the jobs in America," said Cantor.

In Europe, such firms play a similar size role in their nation's economies. Small businesses account for 60 percent of all jobs in France, 67 percent of the workforce in Spain, and 80 percent of Italy's workers. Because these SMEs do not issue bonds or sell equity in public markets they rely largely on banks for financing. And since SMEs are so vital, they are dependent on how cleanly interest rates are set by the Central Banks and feed through to the rates that firms pay. But the Central Banking system seems to have broken down globally. Data suggests the possibility of a depression in Spain and Italy severe enough to plunge the entire Euro zone into a much deeper crisis. Some solutions are being implemented. In the United Kingdom, the Bank of England offers banks $16 of funding assistance for every $1 of new loans to SMEs. An even bolder move would be for the Central Bank to buy SME loans directly from banks. The alternative of a Euro zone depression is far worse.[1]

As a template for other economies, both developed and emerging, VC is also growing in importance and has become a key catalyst in driving GDP growth, employment, personal income, and industrial production. Venture capital activity has a significant impact on all global economies. Venture capital is a catalyst for job creation, innovation, technology advancement, international competitiveness, and increased tax revenues. As a proxy for innovation within the economic sector, every year there are nearly 2 million businesses created in the United States. According to the 2011 Venture Impact study, produced by IHS Global Insight, VC-backed companies accounted for 11.87 million jobs and over $3.1 trillion in revenue in the United States (based on 2010 data). Those totals are equivalent to 21 percent of GDP and 11 percent of private sector employment.[2]

More Economic Benefits

Additional anecdotal evidence of venture capital's impact on the U.S. economy and financial markets includes the fact that the technology sector at large is now the majority component of the S&P 500's market capitalization. This is a significant increase from the mid-1980s when it was comprised of less than 55 companies. As evidence of the eye-popping potential of venture capital, 80 percent of all initial public offerings (IPO), mergers and acquisitions (M&A), and venture capital investing dollar activity since J.H. Whitney & Company (JHW) was founded in 1946 took place in the two-year tech boom leading up to the 2000 tech bust.

There were 435 M&A transactions of VC backed companies with an aggregate disclosed value of $21B in 2012; a 12.5 percent year-to-year decrease. Forty-nine VC-backed companies went public in 2012, raising $21.4B; a 100 percent year-to-year increase. Moore's Law is still very relevant and features prominently in recent news stories about the exponential increase in semiconductor memory capacity and technological innovation.

Venture capital investment has been almost singlehandedly responsible for delivering huge productivity gains to the U.S. economy by way of financing new information, communication technologies, and innovations. This contributed to a rapid advancement and acceptance in the emerging markets, where it has had a major impact on scaling manufacturing into their economies.

Start-Up Business Benefits

A November 2011 press release from the Kauffman Foundation revealed a survey showing that 54 percent of 18–34-year-olds in the United States want to start a business. When broken down by ethnicity or race, an even higher percentage of young people of color expressed a desire to start their own companies: 64 percent of Latinos and 63 percent of African-Americans. Of those who said they were interested in becoming entrepreneurs, an impressive 18 percent actually tried to start a new business in the United States. This entrepreneurial endeavor was bested only by Australia, which had a 20 percent startup rate within the same demographic. Even in the Middle East, females beat the West as tech founders. Only 10 percent of tech entrepreneurs across the world are women where the average is 35 percent in the Middle East.

Venture capital is one way in which you, as an entrepreneur, can build your company using other people's money (OPM). The venture capitalist provides the capital to allow you to complete development or commercialization of your product, the expertise to help you prove the concept in the marketplace, and the management experience to guide you in growing your business into a profitable enterprise. In exchange, the venture capitalist takes a percentage of ownership or equity in your company.

The ultimate goal of the venture capitalist is not altruism. It is that your company increases in value and ultimately has a liquidity event such as an initial public offering (IPO) to turn it into a public company that sells shares of stock, or a trade sale—a merger or acquisition (M&A) in which another company purchases or merges with your company. In either case, the VC is hoping to realize a substantial return on the capital and other resources invested. It is usually a pretty safe bet that the VC who is backing your startup is doing so because he or she has already been where you are going. They have already determined the probability of success and have a pretty good idea where the pitfalls are and how to avoid them. It is the wise entrepreneur who learns to trust the wisdom the VC brings to the table.

It is also a way in which public and private actors can construct an institution that systematically creates networks that allow new firms and industries to progress. This institution helps in identifying and combining pieces of companies, like finance, technical expertise, marketing experience, and an intimate knowledge of various business models. Once integrated, these enterprises succeed by becoming nodes in the search networks for designing and building products in their domain.[3]

Social Benefit of New Technology and Innovation

Reflect on the following examples of new technologies and innovations and how they impact the way we interact daily with business, family, and friends. If the notion of any of these technological breakthroughs seems farfetched, remember that the TV and heavier than air flying machines once did too! Whether these emerging companies someday grow to the size of a Fortune 500 corporation on their own or are acquired for their groundbreaking products, most all rely on the venture capital industry to get their start.

Medical Innovations

Many of the nation's most innovative medical breakthroughs have been brought to market by billions of dollars of venture capital investment in life sciences companies. The economic impact and medical contributions of these life sciences companies have been enormous. Venture capital investors seek and invest in the most promising therapies and technologies to combat costly and too often fatal chronic conditions such as heart disease, cancer, stroke, and diabetes. Venture investment allows small startup life sciences companies to develop these technologies and commercialize them so that millions of Americans can have access to the most advanced treatments available.[4]

The revolutionary medical breakthroughs produced by VC backed companies such as Amgen, Genentech, Genzyme, Gilead Sciences, Kyphon, Intuitive Surgical, and Scimed Life Systems, along with hundreds of smaller innovative life sciences companies, amount to highly tangible and valuable improvements to the U.S. economy and to people's lives. Today, small venture backed companies often serve as the research and development (R&D) pipeline for the larger life sciences corporations who seek to acquire the most promising innovations.[5]

The good news for today's baby-boomers is that medical celebrity Dr. Mike Roizen, Chief Wellness Officer for the esteemed Cleveland Medical Clinic, has postulated that by 2023, any one of 14 areas of aging research might see a breakthrough allowing us to live to 160 with the same quality of life we enjoy at 45! Thank you, VC!

Finally, a lot is written about the plusses and minuses of the 2,300+ page Affordable Health Care Act (AHCA), commonly referred to as "Obamacare." With healthcare-related expenses accounting for 17.9 percent of U.S. GDP, and no doubt some real change to come in how healthcare is delivered, I would postulate that the single biggest impact on lowering costs will be the coming medical breakthroughs in the next 10 years, financed in large part by VC investment.

Casual Games

Signia Venture Partners (SVP) is an early-stage fund that makes investments in mobile, gaming, online video, and education technology. In June 2013, they began raising a $100 million fund to support the public's habit of playing games. SVP was formed by Playdom Inc. founder Rick Thompson. He sold Playdom to Disney for $763.2 million in 2010 and two years later formed SVP with fellow tech industry veterans Dan Fiden, Ed Cluss, and Sunny Dhillon in 2012. They started with $20 million of their own money for the first fund.

SVP is based in Menlo Park, California. Thompson is a prolific tech investor who has found a way to leverage doing what he loves into a successful career. Thompson enjoys playing poker and chess, but he has been an investor and entrepreneur since 1995 and took note of the viral growth of digital games with companies like Zynga.

He follows a founder-investor business model and gets closely involved with the early-stage companies with whom he works. His "hand in glove" approach has led to exits valued in excess of $5 billion during his career. His protégés are considered the next generation of game companies and include startups like mobile gaming firm Funzio, which Gree bought in 2012 for $210 million. Zynga acquired another company funded by Thompson, spending $3.8 million for Wild Needle, a company that focused on games aimed primarily at women. Thompson invested in Wild Needle originally because he recognized that mobile gaming is becoming a larger opportunity and it was one of the game startups that had a "mobile first" strategy. Other startups in that genre, which he is mentoring, include Idle Games, Red Robot Labs, Grand Cru, Rumble Entertainment, Project Slice, Fun+, Airy Labs, Noise Toys, Viki, Social Shield, Udemy, Triangulate, AdChina, and Iddiction.

Thompson is considered to be the Game Master in the VC world. In a recent interview with GamesBeat, the online subsidiary of VentureBeat dedicated to covering the gaming world, Thompson said he had invested in mobile gaming because no one was dominating the market.

"The challenge in a changing game market," said Thompson, "is to get on the new horse and get up to speed as the other one starts to wear down. That certainly creates pressure on companies. The good news is that people are spending a lot more time gaming than they were previously."

He also saw that the solutions to the challenges faced by game developers had applications across many other entrepreneurial startups. He said that he preferred to invest in multiple game companies because that gives him a much better feel for the state of the market, in contrast to investors who make maybe one investment in games.[6]

3D Printing

The economic impact of 3D printing is immense. By merely suggesting the potential promise to bring manufacturing jobs back to the United States, this technology is already having influence on U.S. trade accounts and underscoring the economic power of venture capital investing.

In 1986, Chuck Hull founded 3D Systems in Valencia, California. While watching a flatbed plotter produce a large CAD-generated print of a schematic diagram, Hull had an epiphany and the solid imaging process known as 3D printing or stereolithography became a commercial reality. Along with that came the niche industry of rapid prototyping, the STL file format, and the registration of more than 60 patents covering every fundamental aspect of today's additive manufacturing technologies. Although initially ignored as a fringe technology, this startup is beginning to be recognized as significant as the 1976 startup of the little computer firm formed by the two Steves—Jobs and Wozniak—in the Jobs family garage on Crist Drive in Los Altos, California.

Traditional manufacturing methods, machining in particular, use what has come to be called "subtractive" methods in which material is typically removed from the base stock by cutting, planning, filing, or grinding. Even though fabrication can be considered "additive" because of such processes as joining plates, sheets, forgings, and rolled work via riveting, screwing, or welding, it did not include the information technology component of model-based definition until the recent development of CAD/CAM, computer-aided design and computer-aided manufacturing, and digital process controllers.

"Additive" manufacturing takes virtual blueprints from CAD or animation modeling software and creates digital cross-sections for the machine to successively use as a guideline for printing. Material is deposited on the build bed or platform until material/binder layering is complete and the final 3D model has been "printed." To perform a print, the machine reads the design and lays down successive layers of liquid, powder, paper, or sheet material to build the model from a series of the cross-sections, which correspond to the virtual cross sections from the CAD model, fusing them together to create the final shape. The primary advantage of this technique is its ability to create almost any shape or geometric feature. Printer resolution, which determines the layer thickness and X-Y resolution in dpi (dots per inch), is typically around 100 micrometers (μm) with the individual particles measuring between 50 to 100 μm in diameter.

Using additive manufacturing processes, machines popularly known as 3D or three-dimensional printers can run unattended 24 hours per day, 7 days per week. The printers require an occasional visit from a supervisor to top them up with the powdered materials they use as their "inks," or to remove a completed item, but apart from that they can be left on their own. They build up the objects they are making one layer at a time, as the ink is sintered into place with a laser in a way that creates little waste and can make shapes impossible to achieve using the traditional "subtractive" technology of lathes, milling machines, and cutting tools.

Western research and development companies developed the process; however, China is beginning to utilize the process in manufacturing parts from toys to aircraft structural members.

One of the country's largest 3D printers is 12 meters long and produces titanium fuselage frames and high-strength steel landing gear—objects that require the metal they are made from to be free of flaws, which might cause them to fail. Although it is still a long way from replacing mass manufacturing, the technology is changing the way products are developed and made.[7]

A side benefit of this technology is that it is bringing formerly outsourced jobs back to U.S. manufacturers, underscoring the economic power of VC.

Orbital in Orbit

On May 25, 2012, a California firm called SpaceX made the first privately run supply mission to the International Space Station (ISS). It was a vindication of NASA's decision to outsource such missions to the private sector and opened up a vast universe of possibilities for the forward-thinking VC investors in today's space race. On April 21, at NASA's Wallops flight center in Virginia, another rocket built by another firm—Virginia-based Orbital Sciences—lifted off from the pad. Admittedly, the flight was only an initial test. The Antares went nowhere near the ISS itself. Nor was it carrying one of Orbital's Cygnus space capsules, which, if all proceeds according to plan, will one day perform the actual docking with the ISS. But it is an important step: If everything continues to go well, then a Cygnus test flight may take place in a few months' time, and Orbital's first ISS resupply mission could happen before the end of the year.

The firm has a $1.9 billion contract with NASA to fly eight cargo missions to the station. That makes it pricier than SpaceX, which will fly 12 missions (two of which it has already completed) for $1.6 billion. But the competition ought to be a good thing for both companies.[8] It certainly opens up a vast universe of possibilities for the forward-thinking venture capital investor.

Social Media

The global impact of social media has created a paradigm shift in how we communicate. Whether measured by the impact on U.S. presidential elections, the effect of the Occupy Wall Street movement, or its serving as the tool to spark the Arab Spring movement, the impact has been and will continue to be far reaching.

It was over in less than three minutes. At 1:08 P.M. on April 23, 2013, a fake tweet from a hacked Associated Press account asserted that explosions at the White House had injured Barack Obama. Stock prices immediately dropped, wiping more than $130 billion off the value of the S&P 500. That understates the severity of the episode, since in many cases liquidity simply disappeared altogether.

It was the first Twitter crash and, as is often the case with Twitter, it was brief and superficial. The Associated Press itself was quick to clarify that the original report was false. This was echoed by the White House. Markets recovered, ending up for the day.

The potential for social media to move markets has increased recently, after a report by the Securities and Exchange Commission enabled companies to use services such as Twitter and Facebook to report news. Bloomberg recently announced that it was integrating Twitter feeds into its terminals.

Computerized trading algorithms that scan news stories for words like "explosions" may have proved less discerning and triggered the sell-off. That suggests a need for more sophisticated algorithms that look for multiple sources to confirm stories.[9]

The more we become interconnected through social media, the greater the possibility exists for us to become more and more alienated and isolated. It is estimated that more than 70 percent of the world's population utilizes the Internet to access information and 20 percent of those use it to meet people. A growing phenomenon called "catfishing," meaning to have a fake online profile, is causing a crisis in confidence in the information that is being presented. This creates a tremendous opportunity for investment in companies who come up with ways to quickly, efficiently, and economically validate information that is presented online as well as protecting data which needs to remain secure.

Cyborgs

The Cyborgs are coming!

These are powered exoskeletons, like the HULC (Human Universal Load Carrier), coming soon from Lockheed Martin. The HULC's initial intention is to help soldiers in combat carry a load of up to 200 pounds at a top speed of

10 miles per hour for extended periods of time. It's amazingly flexible. The system allows the user to run, walk, kneel, crawl, and even squat. It may be strictly military today, but the vast potential for enhancing human capabilities means that it won't be long before it's adapted to civilian tasks.

Google Glass represents a giant step along the path that futurists like Kevin Warwick think is inevitable. That future belongs to the cyborgs. Warwick believes that once our brains are enhanced with powerful implanted electronic processors and we are neurally linked to the global Net, our descendants will enjoy upgraded memories, sensory expansion, enhanced communication capabilities, and much more, all without losing their human qualities. Somewhere Ray Kurzweil must be grinning from ear to ear.

While we are not yet advanced enough to start implanting tiny quantum chips in our brains, we are entering a precursor era—that of the wearable computer.[10]

Future of the Car

What was once one of the largest and most important industries contributing to the U.S. GDP, the automotive industry now accounts for only 4 to 5 percent—6 percent if one includes auto parts. That is about to change dramatically as technological breakthroughs and VC investment help an industry transform itself into a twenty-first century competitor.

Today the car seems poised for another burst of evolution. Granted, battery-powered cars have disappointed; but car companies are investing heavily in other clean technologies. Future motorists will have a widening choice of super-efficient petrol and diesel cars, hybrids (which switch between batteries and an internal-combustion engine), and models that run on natural gas or hydrogen.

Meanwhile, a variety of "driver assistance" technologies are appearing on new cars, which will not only take a lot of the stress out of driving in traffic but also prevent many accidents. More and more new cars can reverse-park, read traffic signs, maintain a safe distance in steady traffic, and brake automatically to avoid crashes. Some carmakers are promising technology that detects pedestrians and cyclists, again overruling the driver and stopping the vehicle before it hits them.

As sensors and assisted-driving software demonstrate their ability to reduce accidents, regulators will move to make them compulsory for all new cars. Insurers are already pressing motorists to accept black boxes that measure how carefully they drive. These will provide a mass of data that is likely to show that putting the car on autopilot is often safer than driving it. Computers never drive drunk nor get distracted by texting, noisy children in the back seat, or a spilled cup of coffee in the lap.[11]

To those naysayers to whom all of this seems only remotely possible if not impossible, I share this personal anecdote. While with Prutech VC in 1985, I led a seed investment of a little over $2 million into a Menlo Park-based company called

Navigation Technology, Inc., the forerunner to today's GPS. The firm was eventually sold to Philips in the early 1990s and went public as NAVTEQ. In late 2007, Nokia announced that it would acquire NAVTEQ in a deal valued at an estimated $8.1 billion! Seeds planted and properly tended do grow.

The Cashless Society

The rapid growth of substitutes for cash, particularly debit and credit cards, has led economists to predict the advent of the "cashless society." With domestic cash holdings amounting to roughly $2,250 per capita, we are still far from a cashless society.

If you Google "cashless society" you get about 600,000 references in under a second, and 20 pages into the references there are still articles on a future world where physical cash is no longer needed. Some see it as a sign of the "end times," some as a capitalist plot, some as a frightening vision of socialists and ever-bigger governments, and some as a logical step in the evolution of a technologically driven international commerce. Some of the cashless society references are showcase articles for the latest innovation that turns your phone or smart card into a functional wallet. The Bitcoin phenomenon (28 million sources on Google!) is a libertarian enthusiast's dream of not just a cashless society but a society with no need for fiat money and central banks.[12]

Robodiptera

Miniature flying robots have been developed that are no bigger than a fly and can now observe and record a situation virtually unseen. The successful flight of these miniature surveillance platforms was recently reported in *Science* magazine. The size of crane flies wingtip to wingtip measure 3 cm and weight 80 milligrams. Beyond military use, civilian applications include search and rescue or pollinating crops. Pratheev Sreetharan co-developed a radically new manufacturing technique with J. Peter Whitney. Both are doctoral candidates, as of this writing, at the Harvard School of Engineering and Applied Sciences (SEAS). Along with their colleagues in the Harvard Microrobotics Laboratory at SEAS, they have been working for years to build bio-inspired, bee-sized robots that can fly and behave autonomously as a colony. Appropriate materials, hardware, control systems, and fabrication techniques did not exist prior to the RoboBees project, so each must be invented, developed, and integrated by a diverse team of researchers. The end result is a flying machine about the size of a penny. In 2009, the National Science Foundation established a funding grant for the program that would provide $2 million per year for five years.[13]

Financial Benefits to Investors

From the VC investor's perspective, the primary consideration in making VC investments is to gain additional incremental investment returns to their portfolio, commensurate with the additional risk exposure. Historically, the targeted investment return objective has been a 20 to 30 percent compounded return, resulting in an additional 500+ basis points of incremental return to an investor's portfolio. According to Cambridge Associates, VC net annual returns have outstripped the S&P 500 by 8.6 percentage points from 1980 through 2012. (See Table 3.1.)

Accel Partner's $12.7 million Facebook investment in 2005 created a $2 billion windfall when the stock was sold by Accel in the IPO. The joint Kleiner, Perkins, Caufield, & Byers and Sequoia $20 million investment in Google became a $3 billion return *each* four years later. These mind-boggling VC investment returns are certainly *not* events that occur often, but happen often enough to continue to lure VC investors to invest in the space.

The Power of VC's Multiplier Effect

So now you have an appreciation for the "multiplier impact" of VC. Not only VC investors benefit from venture capital's financial rewards. There is also very meaningful economic and social benefits from VC investing for the recipient companies in terms of the employees working for the VC-funded companies, as well as their respective communities, and institutions and infrastructure where the VC companies are located.

Table 3.1 U.S. Venture Capital Fund Index Summary End-to-End Pooled Return, Net to Limited Partners

Index	1-Q	1-YR	3-YR	5-YR	10-YR	15-YR	20-YR	25-YR	30-YR
Cambridge Associates LLC U.S. Venture Capital Index®[1]	1.15	7.17	11.37	4.06	6.87	24.71	28.46	19.27	17.11
U.S. Venture Capital — Early Stage Index[1]	1.03	8.85	11.96	4.07	5.75	68.84	39.97	24.64	20.50
U.S. Venture Capital — Late & Expansion Stage Index[1]	1.89	3.33	14.74	7.29	10.97	8.56	11.77	11.93	12.03
U.S. Venture Capital — Multi-Stage Index[1]	1.08	5.86	9.33	2.88	7.61	6.69	13.52	11.69	11.22
Barclays Government/Credit Bond Index	0.38	4.82	6.71	6.06	5.25	6.03	6.42	7.27	8.08
Dow Jones Industrial Average	-1.74	10.24	10.87	2.62	7.32	5.81	9.65	10.76	11.94
Dow Jones U.S. Small Cap Index	3.69	19.46	13.52	5.25	10.98	7.88	9.98	NA	NA
Dow Jones U.S. TopCap Index	-0.10	10.77	11.03	1.94	7.56	4.64	8.17	NA	NA
Nasdaq Composite*	-3.10	15.91	9.99	2.63	8.50	4.46	7.76	9.25	8.92
Russell 1000®	0.12	16.42	11.12	1.92	7.52	4.75	8.35	9.89	10.80
Russell 2000®	1.85	16.35	12.25	3.56	9.72	5.89	8.43	9.74	9.55
S&P 500	-0.38	16.00	10.87	1.66	7.10	4.47	8.22	9.71	10.78
Wilshire 5000 Total Market	0.10	16.05	11.15	2.03	7.85	4.86	8.30	9.78	10.61

Source: Cambridge Associates LLC, "U.S. Venture Capital Index® and Selected Benchmark Statistics," December 31, 2012, 3. Used with permission.

Another by-product of the multiplier effect is how the financial successes of entrepreneurs are again repeated by their desire to return to center stage with yet a new start-up. There are many instances of two-, three-, and four-time repeat entrepreneurs becoming angel and venture capital investors. These success stories are some of the most valuable contributors to the VC ecosystem and the U.S. economy.

Sowing the Seed

Imagine, if you will, a time a few years in the future. A group of young and very talented researchers from disparate fields have been brought together through social media and their shared interest in *Star Trek*. They are standing together on the balcony overlooking the floor of the New York Stock Exchange preparing to ring the closing bell, after which they will take limousines uptown to a private reception celebrating the multibillion dollar IPO of their company, RecomTek. The firm's new medical scanner, the Recombinator 2020, is a sophisticated integration of infrared cold laser nano-sintering, holographic imaging, genetic engineering, and precision robotic guidance systems, which can repair damaged tissue, restore worn or damaged cartilage, and remove previously inoperable malignancies all while correcting defects in the patient's DNA code. Their new enterprise was made possible by a foresighted venture capitalist who has just finished reading this chapter.

Chapter Four

Prevailing Investment Climate

Your house is on fire, and you're smoking in bed!

—Billy Tauzin, U.S. Representative,
Louisiana Third District, 1985–2005

LIKE MOST ASSET classes, timing is everything. Sometimes, this is preordained by way of making the right decisions, and sometimes it's just pure luck. Either way, I'll take it. Coming out of the 2007–2008 recession and entering into the ensuing investment climate, which featured near

0 percent interest rates, higher taxes, and more regulation, our raison d'être at GCA is to control the destiny of our investments. In order to be sure we are able to pay the higher taxes imposed upon our invested capital, we strive to make outsized returns on invested capital. That is easier said than done.

As a result, we launched the latest in our vintage series of venture capital funds in late 2012. The GCA Catalyst Fund is in fact an inflection point fund, hence the name "catalyst," which we reset or rebooted to achieve the near impossible. Catalyst seeks to back serially successful repeat entrepreneurs who can demonstrate business plans with milestone roadmaps that are capable of achieving a critical mass of operating, financing, and strategic value such that they are positioned to consider a possible liquidity event within 18 months. Yes, you heard right, I said within 18 months. Moreover, we are looking for minimum cash-on-cash returns of more than 10×!

This VC investment strategy obviously doesn't work for every business plan—in fact not even for most; however, it works for those who meet our prevailing economic climate-adapted investment criteria. Most important is our ability to identify companies where we invest not just financial capital, but, equally important, our intellectual capital. This includes our time, sector skill set, wisdom forged from experience, and the company-relevant relationship Rolodex to go with it. If aligned properly, this combination will materially enhance our portfolio company entrepreneur's prospects of success. I truly believe that, irrespective of the challenges faced in prevailing investment climates, it is possible to succeed, provided the VC investor and their portfolio companies adapt in an appropriate manner.

View of Prevailing Investment Climate

Our present economic situation is unparalleled in American history. Real GDP growth rates for each decade from 1790 to 2012 reveals the sluggishness of our present economic environment. The 1.8 percent average rise this century pales in comparison to the 3.8 percent growth rate since 1790. Only the 1930s growth rate was worse! The current and forward-looking economic and investment climate depends, more than any other time in our history, on the policy makers and their accurate interpretation of the facts and their understanding of the underlying drivers.

It is not my intention to indict public policy or put forward a political conclusion. My interest is solely in presenting the facts and putting forward the economic and investment ramifications. The specific recommendations made are an attempt to find true north and suggest remedies to correct some of the problems which threaten to discourage opportunities for our economy's two most important drivers—SMEs and VCs.

As Harvard professors Josh Lerner, Ann Leamon, and Felda Hardymon point out, policy makers are acutely interested in the venture capital industry and monitor it closely. They have a compelling interest to regulate the industry, to protect the general economy from the "problematic practices" of large buyout funds and hostile takeovers; but at the same time, they must encourage the industry to invest more in young firms that are developing promising technologies with enormous social impact and helping to create jobs.[1]

We are, unfortunately, in the proverbial Red Zone. The U.S. economy is like a patient suffering from congestive heart failure and running out of options and time. It does not have the latitude of extra time or spare capacity, like previous post–World War II recession periods, where our baselines gave us additional flexibility. As such, we are operating in an investment environment akin to a live powder keg that could ignite with the slightest provocation and set off a chain of events that no one wants to see: credit defaults, bankruptcies, credit downgrades, higher levels of real unemployment, civil unrest, and the accompanying unraveling of the internationally-intertwined bond markets.

The near-to-intermediate-term negative impact of doing nothing is, in my opinion, magnified by both our untested monetary policy and lack of fiscal policy leadership. This, coupled with the unprecedented and extraordinarily high levels of government and household debt and historically low levels of household savings, has distorted or created the illusion of record corporate profits and earnings multiples. This is another economic bubble that is quickly reaching the point of being ready to burst like a tsunami across the financial landscape.

Not only does today's Shiller P/E of 24.4 (about the same level as the record high recorded in August 1929) suggest a seriously overvalued market, but the rapid multiple expansion of the last two years in the absence of earnings growth suggests that this market is also seriously overbought.[2]

John Mauldin, renowned financial expert and New York Times *best-selling author*

We can no longer allow policy makers to just kick the can down the road and avoid dealing with the fundamental causes of the coming economic implosion. That would be extremely reckless and irresponsible. Addressing this Red Zone will require some heavy lifting and major multi-tasking decisions regarding a host of related investment climate ecosystem issues. One of two things needs to happen very soon. The first is proactive and will require political leadership that is truly bipartisan and courageous enough to abandon ideology and enact tested and proven fiscal policies that would, at this late stage, prove painful and unpopular in the short-to-intermediate run. Given the modus operandi of the cast of characters currently running the show in Washington, DC, both Democrat and Republican, that course of action seems improbable.

The second, more reactionary solution is probably going to be the inevitable default scenario. The bond markets will finally draw the line in the sand, as they have in Europe, and the retraction will not be pretty. Unless we have some adult leadership step forward and take decisive action, it is highly improbable that our economy can continue to struggle forward for more than another 12 to 18 months before imploding.

The Detroit bankruptcy is emblematic of the type of catalyst that could set off a chain reaction. It could be the revelation of yet another banking scandal that is brought to light; insiders will tell you that there are many lurking just below the surface. Whatever event serves as the trigger, we are staring at a meltdown that will not only dwarf the Great Depression of the 1930s, but will likely lead to the balkanization of the Republic and widespread civil unrest as the expectations and demands of the entitlement class finally outstrip the willingness of the producers to participate any further in the government's political Ponzi scheme.

That is, granted, the worst-case scenario. In times of crisis, Americans have historically come together and rallied around leaders offering reasoned and rational solutions. To that end, allow me to offer a compass direction for an SME/VC-friendly policy platform of solutions for consideration while we still have time in which to act. I do not believe that we have to accept being in the Red Zone with its anemic 1 percent GDP growth and low job creation. If we can recognize the structural headwinds beating against us, we can set our sails to change course.

The Size of Government Debt

In a column entitled "What Should We Do about National Debt, and When?" published Tuesday, August 17, 2010, by the McClatchy Newspapers Washington, DC, online daily, Kevin G. Hall and Robert A. Rankin clearly defined the government's annual deficit as the gap between tax revenues and the government's spending in a year. The government covers the gap by borrowing, which raises the national debt.

The Heritage Foundation, which tracks U.S. debt (www .heritage.org) shows that the federal debt currently held by the public totals almost $16.4 trillion. The 50 states' debt obligations add another $4.17 trillion (not even counting municipalities), and including the long-term unfunded Social Security and Medicare obligations adds another $48 trillion. And even this does not include other federal obligations in the form of Medicaid or veterans' benefits, for example. A November 2012 column in the *Wall Street Journal* revealed that the sum total exceeds a staggering total of $86.8 trillion, or 550 percent of GDP![3]

The Hall and Rankin column goes on to cite the findings of two prominent economists, Kenneth Rogoff of Harvard University and Carmen Reinhart of the University of Maryland, whose 2009 book, *This Time Is Different*, analyzed 800 years of national financial crises. Their book concludes that when any nation's ratio of government debt to gross domestic product exceeds 90 percent, negative economic consequences commence. These damage GDP growth, which by historical comparison take close to 20 years to fully digest. Today's U.S. debt-to-GDP level is 101.57 percent.[4] Rogoff and Reinhart believe that the United States must reduce its debt or suffer economic stagnation. The adjustment must be controlled and done slowly, they concluded, or it could derail whatever fragile recovery we are currently seeing.[5]

By way of comparison, this debt alarm bell has now been met by countries that represent 75 percent of global GDP. A grimmer reality is that the financial markets do not seem to fully reflect this reality of stunted growth. In my opinion, this represents a psychology typical of irrational market behavior at play.

The Deficit

The federal government needs to enact a balanced budget amendment to the national Constitution similar to ones included in the constitutions of 48 of our 50 states.[6] In order to do this, we should set a 10-year target to balance revenue and spending at the historical peacetime average of 18.5 percent of GDP. Several areas need to be addressed in order to reach this goal.

The first of these is the 600-pound gorilla in the room that nobody wants to talk about, government entitlements. We must first require means testing. Title I, Section 1 of the Social Security Act of 1935 specifically states: "For the purpose of enabling each State to furnish financial assistance, as far as practicable under the conditions in such State, to aged needy individuals. . . ." Social Security was never intended to be a monthly stipend that individuals received simply because they reached a certain age. It was a safety net for "needy" people. If people have retired on a full pension and savings plan that allows them to live above the poverty line, they should not automatically be receiving a monthly Social Security check. Yes, we all have paid into the system; but it was meant to be an insurance policy against reaching an age where you could no longer work and had no other means of income. We can have the debate about how far above the poverty line the cutoff needs to be, but we must all agree that people whose lifestyle places them comfortably in the middle class and above don't need an extra monthly check from us, the taxpayers.

Secondly, we need to raise and, perhaps, even abolish the mandatory retirement age. Again, we have a program, the Age Discrimination in Employment Act of 1967 (ADEA), which is supposed to protect individuals who are 40 years of age or older from employment discrimination based on age. The problem is that it is not being prosecuted. Too many employers are replacing senior employees with less expensive, more technically savvy younger employees as a cost-cutting measure. In far too many cases, these senior employees are sidelined right before their pensions or other retirement obligations are vested. Any employer who voluntarily removes a senior employee should be required to show just cause for the action, even in right to work states, due to the fact that the financial ramifications of the action are often borne by the taxpayers.

Simpson-Bowles

We have brought together very smart people to form commissions, like the Simpson-Bowles Committee, to make recommendations on ways to reduce the government's deficit, and then we allow our political representatives to ignore the recommendations. The plan is a balanced, comprehensive approach that addresses all parts of the budget. In addition to the $2.7 trillion in deficit reduction already enacted, not including sequestration, the new Simpson-Bowles plan would produce a total of $5.2 trillion in deficit reduction, enough to bring the debt down to about 69 percent of GDP by 2023, putting it on a clear downward path as a share of the economy.

Discretionary Caps

There are five key components to the plan. The first of these is to tighten and strengthen discretionary caps to demand additional efficiency from Washington in place of abrupt across-the-board cuts. The recommendation is for this to be done in two steps: first, by restoring 70 percent of the sequestration cuts in 2013 and, second, by limiting the defense and nondefense spending growth to the rate of inflation through 2025. The dirty little secret about budget cuts in Washington, DC, especially with the sequestration, is that the "cuts" were not in any actual budgets. They were in the percentage of the automatic increase in the budget. In other words, if a department was budgeted to spend $8 million this year and their budget for next year was scheduled to increase to $10 million, it would be a 25 percent increase in the real world. If they were only authorized to spend $9.5 million, it would be an increase of 18 percent in the real world. Only in Washington, DC, is this considered a draconian 7 percent budget cut. As Charles Grodin so brilliantly summed up the federal budget to Kevin Kline in the 1993 movie *Dave,*

I just think they make this stuff a lot more complicated than it has to be.

Federal Health Spending

The second recommendation is to reform federal health spending. This would include means testing for financially better-off beneficiaries, reducing fraud and abuse at all levels of the healthcare system; modernizing cost-sharing rules with new cost protections; gradually increasing the Medicare age with a buy-in at age 65; and re-orienting incentives for doctors, hospitals, lawyers, and beneficiaries to improve the delivery of health care and truly bend the cost curve. These reforms would remove the insurance company from between the doctor and the patient, change the way hospitals are allowed to depreciate equipment costs, and introduce meaningful tort reform that would significantly reduce the number of frivolous medical malpractice suits that are filed every year.

Additional Spending Cuts

The third recommendation of the committee was to identify additional spending cuts to reduce various government subsidies in areas like farming, education, and commerce. Various cuts were identified by modernizing the military and civilian health and retirement systems, improving the financial state of the Pension Benefit Guaranty Corporation (PBGC), modernizing the management and operations of the postal service, and eliminating all congressional earmarks.

Tax Reform

Fourth, enact comprehensive tax reform that uses a "zero plan" model as a starting point to dramatically reduce the size and number of tax expenditures in the code, sharply reduce rates, improve overall simplicity, and move toward a territorial system to promote growth and generate revenue. Tax reform should be written by the committees but enforced with an across-the-board tax expenditure limitation.

Accountability

Finally, the Simpson-Bowles Committee suggested that the federal government implement government-wide reforms to reduce waste, fraud, and abuse. The federal government needs to modernize their means and methods for more accurately measuring inflation. This data should be reflected within the budget and tax code to provide much-needed protections for low-income individuals and the oldest beneficiaries.

The plan also calls for reforms on a separate track to the Social Security and transportation trust funds to make them sustainably solvent as well as to restrain the growth of federal health care costs. It seeks to reduce long-term deficits in a way that promotes economic growth and protects the most vulnerable.[7]

Give Us Only What We Need

Someone has to break the unwritten bureaucratic rule in Washington, DC, which says that once a federal program is created, it can never be shut down. All federal government programs need to have a sunset provision retroactively attached to them requiring the program to come up for review by an independent, nonpartisan citizen review board every 10 years or so. If the program can no longer be shown to be effectively addressing the issue for which it was created or is no longer financially viable, it should be terminated. This includes even the quasi-government programs like Freddie Mac and Fannie Mae. And there should be strict prohibitions against lobbyists having any contact whatsoever with members of the review board.

We also need real student loan reform. We need to get colleges and universities out of the business of education and back to the mission of education: 37 million young Americans owe $1 trillion in government-sponsored loans, a 300 percent increase in just the past eight years. Many of them have degrees that they will never use in the workplace. Offsetting federal grants to the institutions against tuition hikes would help to make a college education more affordable for a greater number of students and force the institutions to reexamine their priorities. Allowing the 50 states to serve as laboratories for what type of degrees and programs are offered would also bring some accountability back into the system. These are all well intended programs, but the focus should be on those who need them and are phased out by income for those who do not need them.

I would like to see a market-based auction process to privatize all nonessential government assets and services. In tandem, the 50 states can again serve as valuable test laboratories. New Jersey Governor Chris Christie issued an executive order in March 2010 creating the New Jersey Privatization Task Force, a short-lived advisory body established to identify a comprehensive set of privatization tools and strategies the state could apply to save at least $50 million in fiscal year 2010–2011. The New Jersey Privatization Task Force asserted, "States that have had the most success in privatization and have created a permanent, centralized entity to manage both privatization and related policies aimed at increasing government efficiency." A case in point is the 1980 Staggers Act, which deregulated the U.S. freight railways and led to a surge in private infrastructure investment—$511 billion in total, or 17 percent of annual revenues over the ensuing periods, leading to all seven of the largest freight railways reaching profitability in recent years.[8] This government-private sector privatization partnership is so important, that it is the subject matter for my proposed second and final book, *Privatization: Monetizing U.S. Debt to Empower America.*

Changing with the Times

It has been more than 50 years since Congress updated patent law, and its update is critical to American innovation and jobs. Reforms are needed at the U.S. Patent Office (USPTO) if the United States is going to remain a global player in technological innovations. The U.S. Patent Office should be privatized as it is currently a major drag on GDP. Veteran high-tech CEO Henry Nothhaft addressed this issue in his book, *Great Again: Revitalizing America's Entrepreneurial Leadership*, in which he pointed out that it now takes an average of 3.7 years to obtain a patent, from submission of a patent application to award. Some applications can take as long as seven years. The problem is that over the last two decades, Congress has siphoned off over $1 billion in patent application fees to cover budget shortfalls in other areas. In that last 10 years, applications awaiting approval have soared to more than 1.2 million, leaving the understaffed office swamped. Congress would do much toward jump-starting the economy and the VC industry in particular if they would restore the office's funding and make it a market-based, private sector–government partnership, with incentives for performance in processing applications and issuing patents in a timely manner.[9]

Issues of intellectual property ownership, period of ownership, and international enforceability also need to be addressed. The laws need to be changed to prevent large multinational companies from patent squatting. Every year, thousands of independent inventors are discouraged from bringing their products to market because of the threat of litigation for patent infringement by the legal departments of the large companies in the field. This is using the law as a cudgel to intimidate and discourage competition and innovation. This stifles innovation and only benefits the attorneys. This practice must be stopped.

Free trade agreements reduce trade barriers whenever possible and give everyone access to global markets. This helps to foster economic freedom, increase prosperity, and encourage equality for everyone around the world. As such, the government should complete free trade agreements with all World Trade Organization–approved countries. These agreements must include well-defined damages and sanctions for violators. Of ever greater importance is a clear process and punitive fines and trade restrictions for sensitive commercial and national security–related cyber security offenses.

Along with expanding free trade, we need to update and reform our immigration. This is a human rights issue that has been shamelessly hijacked by professional politicos who want to use it as a way to expand their power base. We have the technology to secure the borders and should spend the money for a technology-based infrastructure upgrade. We also need to reform the citizenship process for legal aliens and find a reasonable way to welcome those who are here illegally but who are working. Congress should create a realistic step-by-step approach rather than a single comprehensive proposal, such as a temporary work force program. More than 40 percent of S&P 500 firms were founded by immigrants or their children. This country was built by the wave of immigrants who came to America seeking freedom and opportunity. Last year, we only let in a paltry 225,000 immigrants who possessed some sort of special skills. This is only about 0.1 percent of the labor force. John F. Kennedy tried to impart to us the vision that we are a nation of immigrants, and, to the extent that we can create a climate where we can make immigrants rich, we can all prosper.

The other side of the immigration coin is expatriation. Just as immigration is creating problems in the workforce, expatriation is siphoning off jobs for that workforce as companies move their operations offshore. There are several factors influencing these companies, but first and foremost is the growing burden of the government bureaucracy as evidenced by the thousands of man-hours spent every year simply trying to comply with volumes of regulations by filling out reams of paperwork and countless forms. Many of these regulations have been applied broadly across entire industries, whether or not they had specific application to the company. Some regulations, especially those regarding the environment, are reactionary, have no regard for their economic and social impact, and have no basis in real science. We should allow free-market development of all energy resources—oil, gas, coal, wind, solar, nuclear, and even biomass—while maintaining adherence to environmental standards based upon substantive scientific research and data.

A second factor is the onerous and often incomprehensible tax code of the United States. It is deliberately obtuse to allow the federal government to do central planning and control the economy. There are many who espouse a flat tax across the board on all income, ranging from a low of 10 percent with no loopholes or exceptions all the way up to 19 percent with deductions for mortgages, education, medical, and savings. This would be fine, except that the politicians could still find ways to creep up the tax rate and generate more revenue for the government's coffers. Others endorse scrapping the entire tax-on-income scheme and replace it with a consumption tax. Proponents of the "Fair Tax" point out that when you couple income tax with FICA deductions, their proposal of a 23 percent sales tax is absolutely revenue neutral. Their plan would only tax the purchase of new items, would exempt taxes on necessities such as food and medical expenses, and would have a monthly "prebate" for lower income earners that would help them cover the costs of their basic needs. The Fair Tax plan is the only one that would recover taxes from the underground economy of cash-only businesses, tourist expenditures, and earnings from illicit activities. It would also eliminate the grossly unfair double taxation of estate and inheritance taxes, allowing families to build successful enterprises and pass them on to their progeny. Any changes in the tax rate under this plan would be immediately noticed by the tax payers.

An elimination of tax on income would allow small business owners to take the necessary risks to grow and expand their businesses, creating more jobs, and freeing up the flow of revenue in the economy. Another spur to the economy would be the implementation of a small, flat repatriation tax, which would allow U.S. multinational corporations and individuals who have offshore earnings to bring that money back to the domestic economy without feeling that they were being robbed.

Thirdly, it is about time for us to honestly and objectively evaluate the monetary policy of this government. The monetary policy of the United States of America is managed by the private banking cartel known by the gross misnomer of the Federal Reserve System. There is nothing "federal" about it.

The Fed's original monetary policy objectives at the time of its charter were maximum employment, stable prices, moderate long-term interest rates, and *now* setting targeted GDP growth rates. For the last 100 years under the Fed's management, the purchasing power of the dollar has fallen by more than 90 percent. The Bureau of Labor

Statistics vigorously denies allegations that it has to cook the numbers every month to make the public think that the unemployment rate is in single digits. They allegedly do this by no longer counting the people who have gotten discouraged and either quit looking for work or have used up all of their unemployment benefits. Government apologists say there is nothing wrong with that methodology. According to John Williams, the Dartmouth-educated economist who posts *all* of the government's data on the website Shadowstats.com, there is another side to the story. When the total percentage of the available labor force currently not working is added together, the real unemployment rate is 23.3 percent. That is more than three times higher than the official 7.4 percent rate published at the time of this writing.[10]

Given the recent revelations of institutional disingenuousness in other agencies and departments, it not a stretch to believe that the American people are being misinformed and cozened by the very people who are supposed to be looking out for our best interests. The multinational banks create credit bubbles, and the Fed, itself a member of an international private banking cartel, arranges for them to get bailed out by our tax dollars when the bubbles burst. Only a truly independent arbiter of monetary policy can manage the elusive balance between interest rates and money supply in order to control economic growth, inflation, and unemployment (an objective that is highly debatable in my opinion). That independence has been thoroughly compromised with the revolving doors between the Federal Reserve, Wall Street, and the U.S. Treasury that have developed over the last few administrations. We are hopeful that adherence to the new Basel III accords will go a long way toward achieving the kind of economic certainty that allows for reasonably accurate financial projections and business planning. Abandoning the failed Fed experiment and returning to a resource-backed currency would further strengthen the nation's monetary policy and support renewed economic growth.

In the aggregate, this 10-year public policy initiative would address government debasement and its unintended consequences—*social debasement*. As illustrated by the Cantillon Effect, the 99 percent blame the 1 percent, the 1 percent blame the 47 percent, the private sector blames the public sector, the public sector returns the sentiment, the young blame the old, everyone blames the rich, yet few, if any, question the ideas and policies put forward by the government.

I believe that merely articulating these policies as the U.S. government's 10-year, market-driven mantra would have an exponential impact on the trajectory of improved investor confidence, spending, and hiring practices, which in turn would create drive for renewed vigor in the U.S. economy. The 10 years are important in order to dollar-average our way into implementation and minimize short- to intermediate-term collateral damage. But make no mistake; there will be collateral damage in all cases. That said, this series of bitter pills is the medicine that the patient needs and *now*!

How Investment Climate Affects Start-Ups and Job Creation

Economist Tim Kane authored a study in July 2010 for the Kauffman Foundation, which examined for the first time job creation by newly formed firms, as opposed to small firms, using a new data series from the Commerce Department called Business Dynamics Statistics, which had annual counts of job creation and loss recorded by cohorts of firms by their age from 1977 to the present. The Bureau of Labor Statistics (BLS) issued an almost identical study in August 2010, which used Labor Department data (from 1994 to the present). Both studies affirmed the known fact to all but the "99 percenters" that start-ups create essentially all net new jobs. Existing employers, it turns out, tend to be net job losers, averaging net losses of 1 million workers per year. Entrepreneurial firms create a net 3 million jobs per year on average.

The state of entrepreneurship in the U.S. is, sadly, weaker than ever. There are fewer new firms being formed today than two years ago when the recession ended. As the Bureau of Labor Statistics (BLS) describes: "New establishments are not being formed at the same levels seen before the economic downturn began, and the number is much lower than it was during the 2001 recession."[11]

On July 30, 2013, the Bureau of Labor Statistics issued a press release covering the business employment dynamics for the fourth quarter of 2012. The opening paragraph was blunt.

> From September 2012 to December 2012 gross job gains from opening and expanding private sector establishments were 7.1 million, an increase of 238,000 jobs from the previous quarter, the U.S. Bureau of Labor Statistics reported today. Over this period, gross job losses from closing and contracting private sector establishments were 6.4 million, a decrease of 231,000 jobs from the previous quarter.
>
> www.bls.gov/news.release/pdf/cewbd.pdf

One might expect entrepreneurship to be rising in the United States, especially with lower fixed costs for modern service-based start-ups, as well as other advantages, such as higher levels of human capital, higher incomes, and the rising availability of funding through bank and venture capital.

Based on Kane's initial research into the importance of start-ups for job creation, cited by the 2011 Economic Report of the President, this paper extends that data series by an additional two years. The following figures show how important start-ups are for net job creation. Since 1977, newly born companies usually create a net 3 million jobs per year, but the most recently released data report this number as falling to 2.34 million in the year 2010. The Commerce Department did not release annual 2011 or 2012 data until after the 2012 election, but quarterly figures for start-up job creation have continued to weaken. Adding the quarterly figures in 2010 yields a total of 2.932 million jobs, but in 2011 that sum total dropped to 2.928 million. Kane estimated annual 2011 figures using that as the proxy. CNN released an updated report in October 2012, which showed that the net gain since the current administration took office in January 2009 was only 125,000 jobs.

The next step is to convert that start-up data into a per capita metric. The national population grew from 246 million people to 311 million, according to the U.S. Census. After converting, it is clear that entrepreneurs are having a harder time starting a company today than at any time since the government began collecting data.

The rate of job creation at start-up companies was steady in the 1980s and 1990s at 11 start-up jobs per 1,000 people (i.e., among every 1,000 Americans, 11 were newly hired at a company started that year). But the start-up jobs rate has collapsed in recent years. In fact, the rate of start-up jobs during

2010 and 2011, years that were technically in full recovery, is the lowest on record. The second figure shows how the rate declined during the recession years 2008–2009, but also shows that it continued to decline afterwards. The average rate for entrepreneurial job creation under the previous three presidents was 11.3, 11.2, and 10.8 respectively, but under the current administration it has been cut by one-third to 7.8.

Economic theory suggests that the modern economy offers a better environment for even more entrepreneurship. First, there is a wider technology frontier to explore. Second, a wealthier society enables more individuals to explore diverse opportunities rather than merely work to survive. Third, the shift to services requires less start-up capital than manufacturing or agriculture. In other words, the downward trend in the rate of entrepreneurship should, in theory, have rebounded by now. According to the economist Sander Wenneker, there is an empirically based U-shaped relationship between self-employment and economic development.

Why Is Entrepreneurship Still Declining in the United States?

There is anecdotal evidence that the U.S. policy environment, or lack thereof, has become inadvertently hostile to entrepreneurial employment. At the federal level, high taxes and higher uncertainty about taxes are undoubtedly inhibiting entrepreneurship, but to what degree is unknown. The dominant factor may be new regulations on labor. The passage of the Affordable Care Act is creating a sweeping alteration of the regulatory environment that directly changes how employers engage their workforces, and it will be some time until those changes are understood by employers or scholars. Separately, there has been a federal crackdown since 2009 by the IRS on U.S. employers who hire U.S. workers as independent contractors rather than employees, raising the question of mandatory benefits. This has direct bearing on the VC process as new firms typically use part-time and contract staffing rather than full-time employees during the start-up stage.

According to Labor Department data, the typical American today only takes home 70 percent of their compensation as pay, while the rest is absorbed by taxes and the spiraling cost of benefits (e.g., health insurance). The dilemma for U.S. policy is that an American entrepreneur has zero tax or regulatory burden when hiring a consultant or contractor who resides abroad. But that same employer is subject to paperwork, taxation, and possible IRS harassment if employing U.S.-based contractors. Finally, there has been a steady barrier erected to entrepreneurs at the local policy level. Brink Lindsey points out in his e-book, *Human Capitalism*, that the rise of occupational licensing is destroying start-up opportunities for poor and middle-class Americans.

The quantitative impact of the shifting policies on start-ups and job creation is in need of further study. There is a widespread sense that globalization of the economy exposes companies to new challenges by leveling the playing field for trade. There is no doubt a level playing field among economic institutions as well, where service-based employment can move quickly from one jurisdiction to another. By cracking down on employing Americans part-time, and mandating higher benefits, new American policies may be pushing jobs overseas. This is an issue policymakers must consider carefully when designing rules and regulations for the twenty-first century economy.

Policies for a Vibrant VC Sector

As the voice of the U.S. venture capital community, the National Venture Capital Association (NVCA) advocates for public policies that encourage innovation, spur job creation, and reward long-term investment in start-up companies. By working with the venture capital community to foster a growth environment for emerging businesses, the federal government can help ensure that America maintains its global economic leadership and competitive advantage into the twenty-first century and beyond. Notwithstanding your author's shared public policy panacea, following is a summary of the public policies advocated by the NVCA.

Tax Policy for Long-Term Investments

People who take the risk to invest their capital to start a company, which in turn creates jobs and stimulates positive economic activity, should not have to endure an extortionate shakedown by the government when their venture is successful. NVCA has long advocated for a tax structure that fosters capital formation and rewards long-term, measured risk taking. NVCA believes that the returns earned by venture capitalists and entrepreneurs for building successful companies over the long term should continue to be taxed at the capital gains rate. They continue support for a capital gains tax rate that is globally competitive and preserves a meaningful differential from the ordinary income rate.

As lawmakers consider broad-scale tax reform to create a simpler, fairer tax code, NVCA urges both Congress and the Administration to build a system that supports entrepreneurs and their investors. NVCA will support proposals that meet the criteria above and that take into account the economic value created by the venture capital asset class and the importance of encouraging investment in long-term job creation.

A Vibrant Capital Markets System

Studies show that significant job creation occurs when a venture-backed company goes public. In the last decade, however, the market for venture-backed initial public offerings (IPOs) has suffered. From Sarbanes Oxley (SOX) to the Global Settlement to Reg FD, regulations intended for larger multi-national corporations have raised burdensome obstacles and compliance costs for start-ups trying to enter the public markets. The recently enacted JOBS Act addressed many of these challenges, and the NVCA will work with the appropriate regulatory agencies as the new law is implemented. The NVCA will continue to support regulatory and tax policies that seek to encourage small, emerging growth companies to go public on U.S. exchanges. Such policies promise to bolster the economic recovery, spur job growth, and maintain our global competitiveness.

Research Funding for America's Innovation Economy

Maintaining America's global innovation advantage requires continued federal funding for basic research and development. Discoveries in federal labs and universities remain the germination points for breakthrough ideas that can be commercialized by entrepreneurs and venture investors. The promising new companies that result will drive job creation and economic growth. This unique public-private partnership has delivered countless innovations to the American public and a decisive competitive advantage to the U.S. economy for decades. Therefore, NVCA supports policies that fund basic research across high technology industries, including life sciences, energy, and physical sciences. Programs such as the Small Business Innovative Research (SBIR) program fill the innovation pipeline and must receive robust federal support if America wants to continue to bringing breakthrough technologies to market.

Immigration and Workforce Recruiting

The United States must continue to attract and retain the world's best and brightest minds if it wants to maintain its global economic leadership. For this reason, NVCA supports policies that allow foreign-born entrepreneurs to come to America to build their companies and create jobs in the United States. Proposals such as the Start-Up Visa Act will allow enterprising professionals to come here to develop their ideas and then remain here to build their companies, as opposed to innovating and creating economic value overseas. Further, the NVCA supports a streamlining of the pathway to Green Cards for foreign-born graduate students who wish to remain in the United States upon completion of their studies.

Health Care and Medical Innovation

The U.S. market for biopharmaceuticals and medical devices is one of the most heavily regulated industry sectors in the world. There are many good reasons for this, but we must balance regulation with innovation, a principle that has driven high-quality care for American consumers and competitive advantage for American companies for decades. By putting innovation at the forefront of health care reform efforts and regulatory policy making, we can provide incentives to America's most promising young companies to discover new ways to improve the quality of health care, expand access, and reduce the costs. The NVCA supports policies that streamline the regulatory approval process at the Food and Drug Administration (FDA), particularly for novel technologies, as well as the reimbursement process at the Center for Medicare and Medicaid (CMS). Process improvements at these agencies are critical to encourage investors to take the risk and pursue new medical innovations that will save and improve patients' lives and create U.S. job growth.

Energy and Clean Technology

Innovations in clean technology will revolutionize how we produce and consume energy, reduce carbon emissions from fossil fuels, and strengthen national security. Clean-tech development can also spur U.S. job creation and economic growth for decades to come. Due to the exceptional risks and capital requirements associated with developing clean technologies, U.S. energy policy plays an outsized role in the success or failure of venture-backed clean-tech companies. NVCA supports policies that encourage clean-tech innovation and provide incentives for investing in promising young companies in this sector. Such policies include continued federal funding for early-stage basic research at government labs, support of the Advanced Research Projects Agency-Energy (ARPA-E) program, and the establishment of a Clean Energy Deployment Administration, or CEDA, to help the most promising innovations reach the marketplace.

Cyber Security and Intellectual Property Protection

The intersection of intellectual property, cyber security, and the Internet has emerged as an uneasy nexus for policy makers, particularly after the dramatic defeat of the Stop Online Piracy Act/Protect IP Act (SOPA/PIPA) intellectual property legislation earlier this year. While those measures are unlikely to reemerge for the rest of the year, cyber security is taking a front seat, and has also, for lawmakers, created a surprising stir in the privacy and Internet communities. To a certain degree, all of the cyber security bills under consideration face considerable scrutiny in these three main areas:

1. The information to be shared.
2. The purpose for which the information can be shared.
3. The agencies that will have access to the shared information.

Finding compromise on all three facets will be difficult and time consuming, which could lead to stalemate as the most likely short-term outcome. However, unlike in the SOPA/PIPA debate, cyber security threats present a strong national security concern that both political parties understand is real and that must be addressed. NVCA will be monitoring activity in this area closely.

Summary

In the aggregate, the prevailing investment climate, like those of the past, has its respective challenges, and embedded therein are great VC investment opportunities. That said, the current urgency and baseline to implement a forward-looking constructive investment climate is now dangerously high and short, at a time when the VC growth engine is needed more than ever.

As discussed in prior chapters of this book, there are presently immense and untapped reserves of potential investment opportunities for VC sector investors. Public policy allowing the market to flourish is the best way to enable a VC-friendly investment climate that is a catalyst to small business creation and job growth—it's a win-win formula for everyone!

The need is clear. Why wait for disaster? The future is now.

Chapter Five

Field Guide for VC Investing Options—Nonlisted

Nonlisted VC investment options are today primarily reserved for institutional and accredited LPs. Notwithstanding, this is likely to quickly change in the not too distant future and be an attractive investment option to the population at large, once the SEC rules and guidelines governing the JOBS ACT are clarified—we are all waiting!

—Lou Gerken

IRRESPECTIVE of having knowledge of the nonlisted VC investment landscape, it will always be of paramount importance to right-size/right-fit the VC investment option(s) selected given the prevailing investment climate. To right-size/right-fit requires a sixth sense that only comes to the naturally gifted, the lucky, or, more aptly, through years of time-tested VC investment experience. Even the most knowledgeable investors select their best-of-breed fund managers in selected VC asset classes without really knowing how that VC investment strategy will perform over the ensuing VC fund term. This term is typically 10 years to invest and harvest returns and is known as *blind pool investing*. Notwithstanding this blind pool style of investing, the VC investment mantra has historically been to maintain an allocation to the asset class over time, as it has over the long term proven to perform better than traditional asset classes such as listed stocks and bonds.

Most types of alternative investments are not as liquid as stocks and bonds. These include the asset classes of private equity and venture capital, hedge funds, real estate, infrastructure, and commodities. Most investors prize liquidity because it allows them to feel a sense of direct control, in that they can get in and out of securities without too much friction; but, as evidenced in the stock market crashes in 1987 and 2008, liquidity tends to evaporate just when it is needed most.[1]

I vividly remember the two-year period leading up to the Asian Currency Crisis, which surfaced in July 1997, when our firm spent considerable company treasure and time establishing the $400 million GCA Sino-Asia Infrastructure Fund, a Southeast Asian Infrastructure Private Equity Fund. I recall with pride its being dubbed by some prospective investors as a thinking man's fund. After finally arranging a $30 million lead investor commitment from a U.S. state pension fund, and a $200 million co-investment commitment from our co-manager, a leading Hong Kong–listed conglomerate, we were prepared to complete our carefully crafted financial close. This serendipitously fell on the Friday following Wednesday, July 2, 1997, the inflection point for the Asian Financial Crisis—technically when the Thai Baht was surprisingly devalued! Yes, ouch! Our learning moment here was that sometimes bad things happen that you simply cannot control. You just reflect, lick your wounds, and then move on to the next investment opportunity. As if it was any consolation, with 20–20 hindsight, investments made by our more fortunate contemporaries in the period following the Asian Financial Crisis were done at $0.10 on the dollar and generated enormous returns for investors.

Alternative Investments and Venture Capital

The traditional Graham & Dodd asset classes are broadly defined as investing in cash equivalents (bank CDs, savings accounts, etc.), listed common stocks, and fixed-income securities, also known as bonds. These investments are typically made by either investing directly in an investment security or sponsoring entity or through highly liquid mutual funds and listed exchange-traded funds (ETFs).

Alternative investments or *alternative assets* are terms that include tangible assets such as art, wine, antiques, rare coins and stamps, and financial assets such as commodities (CTF), private equity and venture capital, hedge funds, film production, financial derivatives, oil & gas, and real estate.

In the finance industry, private equity and venture capital are oftentimes collectively referred to as private equity, although they require two distinct investment strategies. Notwithstanding, they are both asset classes consisting of equity/debt investment in operating companies that are not typically traded on a public stock exchange. Each of these two categories has its own set of goals, preferences, and investment strategies; each, however, provides capital to a target company to nurture expansion, new product development, or restructuring of the company's operations, management, or ownership.

Bloomberg *BusinessWeek* magazine has called private equity a rebranding of leveraged buyout firms after the 1980s.[2] Notwithstanding, the most common investment strategies in private equity are leveraged buyouts, venture capital, expansion and growth capital, distressed investments and mezzanine capital, infrastructure, real estate, restructuring, secondaries, fund of funds, and a catch-all category known as "special situations." In a typical leveraged buyout (LBO) transaction, a private equity firm buys majority control of an existing or mature firm. This is distinct from a venture capital investment, in which the investors (typically venture capital firms or angel investors) invest in young or emerging companies.

Traditional Stages of Venture Capital Financing

Let us assume that investments are made by way of venture capital funds, notwithstanding that investments can be made directly into companies (term of trade "direct investments") in any of the following investment stages described:

- Seed stage
- Start-up stage
- Expansion stage
- Bridge/pre-public stage

The number and type of stages may be extended and/or overlap by the individual VC firm's investment strategy or if it deems necessary; this is common. This may happen if the venture fund strategy does not perform as expected due to bad management, investment climate, or market conditions.

A VC firm is not only about funding and lucrative returns; it also offers non-funding value such as industry relationships and management know-how for internal issues as well as for external challenges. As the investment relationship progresses through the various stages, we see a decreasing risk of losing the investment the VC firm has made.

Stage at Which Investment Is Made	Risk of Loss of Capital	Causation of Major Risk by Stage of Development
Seed stage	66.2%	72.0%
Start-up stage	53.0%	75.8%
Second stage	33.7%	53.0%
Third stage	20.1%	37.0%
Bridge/pre-public stage	20.9%	33.3%

The Seed Stage

The seed investment stage is typically financed by entrepreneurial sweat equity, friends of the firm, angel investors, angel funds, or micro-cap VC funds and can typically take the form of founder stock and/or a convertible note instrument. Typically, the company's financing requirement is less than $500,000.

This is where the seed funding takes place. It is considered as the setup stage, where a person or a venture approaches a VC firm or angel investor for funding for their idea/product.

During the seed stage, the person or venture has to convince the investor that the idea/product is worthwhile. The investor will perform due diligence with respect to the technical and the economical feasibility (feasibility study) of the project. In some cases, there is some sort of prototype of the idea/product that may or may not be tested, but it is usually not fully developed. The existence or the necessity of intellectual property (IP) protection is carefully examined and verified. The experience and background of the management team is also given a cursory evaluation. The VC must have a warm, fuzzy feeling about the individuals involved in the project and their individual abilities to perform in their required capacities. If not, the VC will have to augment the management team with individuals who are known, dependable performers.

Finally, the VC team will go over the entrepreneur's financials in microscopic detail. The VC wants to know how much money the entrepreneur needs to succeed, how the money is going to be used, how much revenue the project is going to generate, and what percentage return the VC will make on the investment.

If, after completion of the due diligence, the project is determined to be less than feasible or the investor does not see an adequate return on the required investment, the investor will not consider financing the idea. However, if the idea/product is not directly feasible, but part of the idea is worth more investigation, the investor may invest some time and money for further investigation.

Risks/Benefits

At this stage, the risk of losing the investment is tremendously high, because there are so many uncertain factors. Research performed by J.C. Ruhnka and J.E. Young, entrepreneurship professors at the University of Colorado at Denver, shows that the risk of losing the investment for the VC firm is around 66.2 percent, with the causation of major risk by stage of development being as high as 72 percent.[3] Paradoxically, in a similar working paper published by the National Bureau of Economic Research, Harvard Business School professors William R. Kerr and Josh Lerner teamed up with MIT Professor of Entrepreneurial Finance, Antoinette Schoar, to show evidence that seed/angel-funded start-up companies are in fact less likely to fail than companies that rely on other forms of conventional initial financing. Their research included traditional sources of start-up capital including bank loans, family savings, and investments by friends of the firm's founder.[4]

Another serious consideration at this stage is creating unrealistic expectations for future funding rounds by providing too much capital with no performance milestones attached. Setting the valuation too high in the seed round can end up diluting the original shareholders during subsequent funding rounds if the company does not perform as well as expected.[5]

The Start-Up Stage

The start-up stage is typically invested in by angel funds, micro-cap VC funds and institutional VC funds with very early stage capital allocations and takes the form of a Series-A Preferred round of financing. Here, the typical financing need is less than $2 million.

If the idea/product/process is qualified for further investigation and/or investment, the process will go to the second stage; this is called the start-up stage or may also be known as the early stage. At this point, many exciting things happen. A business plan is presented by the attendant of the venture to the VC firm. A management team is being formed to run the venture.

While the organization is being set up, the idea/product gets its form. The prototype is being developed and fully tested. In some cases, clients are being attracted for initial sales. The management team establishes a feasible production line to produce the product. The VC firm monitors the feasibility of the product and the capability of the management team from the board of directors.

To prove that the assumptions of the investors are correct about the investment, the VC firm wants to see results of market research to see whether the market size is big enough; that is, whether there are enough consumers to buy their product. They also want to create a realistic forecast of the investment needed to push the venture into the next stage. If at this stage, the VC firm is not satisfied about the progress or results from market research, the VC firm may stop funding, and the venture will have to search for another investor(s). When the cause relies on handling of the management in charge, they will recommend replacing (parts of) the management team.

Risks/Benefits

At this stage, the risk of losing the investment is shrinking, because the uncertainty is becoming clearer. The risk of losing the investment for the VC firm is dropped to 53.0 percent, but the causation of major risk by stage of development becomes higher, which is 75.8 percent. This may be explained by the fact that the prototype was not fully developed and tested at the seed stage, and the VC firm may have underestimated the risk involved. Or it could be that the product or the purpose of the product have been changed during development.

If the company has a board of directors, a number of people from the VC firm will take seats on it. This is usually where the venture capitalist and the entrepreneur begin to negotiate the issue of control. If there are multiple VCs involved in the initial round of financing, the magnitude of this issue increases exponentially.

Expansion Stage—Second Round Financing

Most often the institutional VC funds are the front-and-center players in these Series-B Preferred financing rounds. The company financial requirements vary greatly but are generally around $10 million.

At this stage, we presume that the idea has been transformed into a product and is being produced and sold. This is the first encounter with the rest of the market, the competitors. The venture is trying to squeeze between those who are already in place, and it tries to get some market share from the competitors. This is one of the main goals at this stage. Another important point is the cost. The venture is trying to minimize their losses in order to reach the break-even point.

The management team has to be adept and must handle company operations very decisively. The VC firm closely monitors the management capability of the team. This consists of how the management team manages the development process of the product and it reacts to competition.

If at this stage the management team has proven its ability to hold up against the competition, the VC firm will probably give a go-ahead for the next stage. However, if the management team begins to show signs of inexperience or inability to effectively manage the company or successfully compete in the marketplace, the VC firm may suggest a restructuring of the management team and redoing the stage. This can entail replacing or reassigning personnel in the management team, rethinking the concept, reconsidering the market segment, or applying any number of analytical tools to discover the root cause of the failure and to correct it, if possible.

Risks/Benefits

At this stage, the risk of losing the investment continues to drop, because the venture is able to estimate the risk. The risk of losing the investment for the VC firm drops from 53.0 percent to 33.7 percent, and the causation of major risk by stage of development also drops at this stage, from 75.8 percent to 53.0 percent. This can be explained by the fact that there is not much developing going on at this stage. The venture is concentrated in promoting and selling the product. That is why the risk decreases.

That being said, this is usually the fail safe point in the venture. If the VC begins to see evidence that the management team is failing to meet milestones for product development, service rollout, market penetration, or revenue generation due to unrealistic projections, unforeseen market barriers, general incompetence, or a host of other red flags, the VC will cut further funding and move on.

Expansion Stage—Third Round Financing

As with the second round, most often the institutional VC funds are the front and center players in these Series-C

Preferred financing rounds. The company financial requirements vary greatly but are generally around $10 million.

This stage is seen as the expansion/maturity phase of the previous stage. The venture tries to expand the market share they gained in the previous stage. This can be done by selling more of the product or expanding into new markets, and it is usually dependent upon having a good marketing campaign. It is also during this stage that the venture begins to search for efficiencies in production costs and internal processes. A good tool for applying management control is the SWOT analysis. It is used to objectively identify and define the strengths, weaknesses, opportunities, and threats that the venture is facing and to develop a course of action for each, which will maximize the firm's strategic advantage and minimize the risk that the venture faces.

If it is determined by management that the venture can begin expanding, the development and marketing teams begin to investigate follow-up products and services. In some cases, expansion of the life cycle of the existing product/service is also investigated.

During this stage, the VC firm monitors the objectives already mentioned in the second stage as well as the new objective mentioned at this stage. The VC firm will evaluate the effectiveness of the management team's ability to reduce costs. It also analyzes the venture's competitiveness in the marketplace and consumer adoption of follow-on products and services.

Risks/Benefits

At this stage, the risk of losing the investment for the VC firm drops from 20.1 percent down to 13.6 percent, and the causation of major risk by stage of development drops almost by nearly a third from 53.0 percent to 37.0 percent. It is often at this stage that new follow-on products or services are being offered. This must be carefully monitored and analyzed to insure that the original offering is not undercut or that there is not a negative market response. This is because the venture is usually relying on the income stream being generated by the initial product to fund the operation. The risk of losing the investment is still decreasing, but must not be ignored.

The Bridge/Pre-Public Stage

The bridge/pre-public round of financing includes both institutional VC funds and the larger passive financial institutions, such as mutual funds and investment managers, who are seeking to invest in the more mature, pre-IPO companies. In these Series-D Preferred financing rounds, the company financial requirements may approach $100 million.

In general this is the last stage of the venture capital financing process. At this stage, the venture has met or exceeded the VC's forecasted goal of achieving a certain amount of the market share. The main goal of this stage is to achieve an exit or liquidity event for the investors. This is brought about by either taking the venture public or developing an opportunity for a sale through a merger or acquisition (M&A).

Internally, management has to analyze where the product is positioned and if it is possible to attract new market segmentation by repositioning the product or scaling the service. This is also the phase in which to further promote follow-on products and/or services to attract new clients and expand into new markets.

This is the final stage of the process. But most of the time, there will be an additional continuation stage involved between the third stage and the bridge/pre-public stage. There have been some limited circumstances where investors have made a very successful initial market impact and were able to move from the third stage directly to the exit stage. Most of the time, however, the venture fails to achieve some of the important benchmarks for which the VC firms aimed.

Risks/Benefits

At this final stage, the risk of losing the investment still exists; however, compared with the numbers mentioned at the seed stage the risk is far lower. The risk of losing the investment in the final stage is a little higher at 20.9 percent. This is caused by the number of times the VC firms may want to expand the financing cycle, not to mention that the

VC firm is faced with the dilemma of whether to continuously invest or not. The causation of major risk during this stage of development is 33 percent. This is caused by the follow-on product or service that is being introduced.

Traditional VC Funds Active in 2012

Accel Partners

Accel Partners (www.accel.com) was founded in 1983 by Arthur Patterson and Jim Swartz. Both are still active investors with the firm. Patterson's successful exits include Applied Micro Circuits, MetroPCS, Veritas, and iPass. Jim Swartz has been responsible for a host of infrastructure, software, and telecommunication launches, including Agile Networks (acquired by Lucent Technologies), Ingenuity Systems, Netlink, and Vitalink.

Other general partners at the firm include Andrew Braccia, Jim Breyer, Sameer Ghandi, Theresia Gouw, and Ryan Sweeney. Recent investments by the firm have included such modern household names as Facebook, Dropbox, Spotify, StumbleUpon, TRUSTe, HootSuite, and Light-Speed.

According to their website (www.accel.com), the firm partners with businesses that show potential for significant long-term success in the specific sectors of infrastructure, Internet and consumer services, mobile, and software and cloud-enabled services. As of this writing, Accel Partners is leading a $1.8 million investment in Collegefeed, a service that combines crowdsourcing with social networking to connect students with each other and potential employers.[6]

Andreessen Horowitz

Andreessen Horowitz (http://a16z.com) is a Menlo Park, California, VC firm founded in 2009 by Marc Andreessen and Ben Horowitz. The company was ranked as the number one venture capital firm by Investor Rank in 2011 and currently has $2.7 billion in assets. Other general partners in the firm include John O'Farrell, Scott Weiss, Jeff Jordan, Peter Levine, and Chris Dixon. The firm is structured differently from most other venture capital firms. Each Andreessen Horowitz partner works on behalf of all its portfolio companies instead of having general partners who specialize in a specific industry.

The company focuses on investments that cover the mobile, gaming, social, e-commerce, education, and enterprise IT (including cloud computing, security, and SaaS) industries. They are most famous for investing $50 million for 2 percent of Skype in 2009, which provided a return of 340 percent when the company was sold just two years later to Microsoft for $8.5 billion. Other ventures of the firm include Twitter, Facebook, Groupon, Instagram, Zynga, Airbnb, and Foursquare.

Benchmark Capital Management

Robert C. Kagle was born and raised by his mother in Flint, Michigan, the onetime vortex of entrepreneurial innovation. Kagle began his business career working at General Motors and received a BS in electrical and mechanical engineering from General Motors Institute (renamed Kettering University) in 1978. He went on to earn his MBA from Stanford Graduate School of Business just two years later. In 1995, he co-founded Benchmark Capital Management (www.benchmark.com) with fellow Rice alumni, Bruce Dunlevie and Kevin Harvey. Benchmark is unusual in that its six general partners share the firm's profits and losses equally, although there have been very few of the latter. Investments have included eBay, Juniper Networks, MySQL, OpenTable, Yelp, Inc., Zillow, Friendster, JAMDAT, Instagram, Hortonworks, Dropbox, Uber, Twitter, Zipcar, Asana, Quora, Gaikai, Demandforce, and DOMO. Since early 2011, Benchmark has had 21 exits, including 7 IPOs and 14 mergers and acquisitions, representing a total market value of more than $9 billion.[7]

Crosslink Capital

Crosslink Capital (www.crosslinkcapital.com) takes a holistic approach to the companies in which it invests its time and talent. Sy Kaufman and Michael Stark founded Crosslink in 1989 with the goal of not only investing in entrepreneurs, but also building long-term relationships that would lead to success. Their expertise is in discovering and managing growth situations, regardless of stage—from two-person, seed-stage private companies to public growth companies with several hundred employees. Crosslink works side by side with management. Their partners have a broad range of both investment and operating management experience. Each investment is staffed with a team of professionals, not just a single partner. This team has access to all the firm's public and private resources to help each of its portfolio companies.

Crosslink invests in five principal sectors: energy technologies, communications services and infrastructure, computing and semiconductors, digital media and Internet services, and software and business services. Their portfolio includes companies such as Ancestry.com, Carbonite, Pandora, and Tivo.

Draper Fisher Jurvetson

DFJ (www.dfj.com/) is a venture capital firm that was founded in 1985. DFJ has backed more than 400 companies in enterprise, software, mobile, clean-tech, energy, healthcare, and other disruptive categories. The Menlo Park firm is currently managing its tenth fund, investing $350 million.

Timothy Cook Draper is the founder. He is a third-generation venture capitalist. His father, William "Bill" Henry Draper III, founded Draper & Johnson Investment Company in 1962, Sutter Hill Ventures in 1968, Draper International India in 1996, and Draper Richards in 2001. His grandfather, William Henry Draper Jr., one of Silicon Valley's first venture capitalists, founded Draper, Gaither, and Anderson in 1959.

John H. N. Fisher is a managing director of DFJ, with 28 years of venture capital investing experience. John has served on the boards of many companies, both private and public. At present, his board positions include SolarCity, Good Technology, CafeMom, SCIenergy, Pulsepoint, and Raydiance.

Steve Jurvetson is a managing director of DFJ. His current board responsibilities include SpaceX, Synthetic Genomics, and Tesla Motors. He was the founding VC investor in Hotmail, Interwoven, Kana, and NeoPhotonics. He also led DFJ's investments in other companies that were acquired for $12 billion in aggregate.

Jennifer Fonstad is a managing director of DFJ and is considered one of the deans of women in venture today. Jennifer invests broadly in early-stage companies with recent investments in mobile applications, consumer and enterprise application services, and energy management. Her investment successes include Athenahealth, Lumenos, Achex, and NetZero.

Khosla Ventures

Vinod Khosla was a co-founder of Daisy Systems and founding chief executive officer of Sun Microsystems, where he pioneered open systems and commercial reduced instruction set computing (RISC) processors. Sun was funded by long-time friend and board member John Doerr of Kleiner Perkins Caufield & Byers. In 1986, Vinod joined Kleiner Perkins, where he was and continues to be a general partner of KPCB funds through KP X. Through the years there, with other partners, he took on Intel's monopoly with Nexgen/AMD. In 2004, Vinod ventured out to create his own venture firm, Khosla Ventures (www.khoslaventures.com/), which invests in a broad portfolio of clean-tech, health-tech, and info-tech start-ups. Khosla Ventures manages five active funds worth more than $2.3 billion.

KV's mission statement is to assist great entrepreneurs who are determined to build companies with lasting significance. The firm is run by people who listen to, analyze, and advise entrepreneurs. They manage a main fund that supports early- and late-stage investments and a seed fund for developing very early-stage experiments. KV focuses on next-generation energy projects, new materials, mobility, the Internet, and silicon technology.

First Round Capital

Not all of the action is in Silicon Valley. In 2004, Josh Kopelman, Howard Morgan, Chris Fralic, and Rob Hayes joined forces to form the Philadelphia-based venture capital firm First Round Capital (www.firstround.com). FRC specializes in seed-stage funding to technology companies. They currently manage two funds: Fund III, launched in October 2010, and Fund IV, launched in April 2012; a total of $261 million is invested in projects ranging between $250,000 to $500,000. This made them one of the busiest VC firms in the country in the last two years. First Round Capital is considered by many in the industry as the third-busiest venture-capital firm in the United States. In 2012, FRC (www.firstround.com) invested in 71 technology companies, placing it behind Silicon Valley-based firms New Enterprise Associates and Kleiner Perkins Caulfield & Byers for total number of investments made in the calendar year.

Versant Ventures

Some VC firms take a path that diverges from technology, the Internet, and software. Versant Ventures (www.versantventures.com) specializes in investments in game-changing medical devices, biopharmaceuticals, and other life science opportunities. They have $1.6 billion under management and are currently investing a $500 million fund raised in July 2008. Their current portfolios include 75 companies and initial investments have been as small as $250,000 and as large as $30 million.

Versant was founded by Brian Atwood, William Link, Donald B. Milder, Barbara Lubash, and Samuel D. Colella.

Atwood specializes in biotechnology investing at Versant. He spent four years at Brentwood Venture Capital, where he led investments in biotechnology, pharmaceuticals, and bioinformatics. He has over 15 years of operating experience in biotech, with an emphasis on therapeutic products, devices, diagnostics, and research instrumentation.

Bill Link specializes in early-stage investing in medical devices at Versant. Prior to co-founding Versant Ventures, he was also at Brentwood Venture Capital. With more than two decades of operations experience in the health-care industry, he has a proven record of building and managing large, successful medical product companies. He has extensive knowledge in ophthalmology.

Don Milder led healthcare investing at CrossPoint Venture Partners prior to Versant. His operating background in healthcare has led him to focus on medical device and healthcare services. He has over 25 years of venture experience as both entrepreneur and investor.

Prior to co-founding Versant Ventures, Barbara Lubash was a partner at CrossPoint Venture Partners. She specializes in healthcare services and information technology at Versant. In her career as an operating executive and venture capital investor, Barbara has led and advised provider, payer, and healthcare IT organizations throughout the United States.

Sam Colella has been a venture capital investor since 1984. Recognized for his leadership in life science investing, he launched one of the first life science venture groups as a general partner at Institutional Venture Partners. Sam has held senior level positions in a diverse array of businesses, including president of Spectra-Physics, the world's leading laser supplier, and senior manager of the technical products division of Corning Glass. He has served as an officer in the National Venture Capital Association, the Western Association of Venture Capitalists, and American Entrepreneurs for Economic Growth. In 2010, he received the Lifetime Achievement Award from the National Venture Capital Association.

The Common Denominator

All of these firms raise the capital for their investment funds from investors known as limited partners (LPs). Each LP looks for a VC who matches their asset allocation strategy based upon the LP's risk tolerance, desired return on investment, and their liquidity requirements.

LPs are typically accredited institutional investors (e.g., pension funds, banks, and insurance companies, endowments and foundations, sovereign wealth funds, family offices, and fund of funds), as well as high-net-worth individuals (HNWIs) with aggregate spousal assets greater than $1 million and annual income greater than $300,000. The minimum investment size required is typically $1 million, subject to waiver by the VC fund management. As such, the traditional, institutional VC funds will not be an asset class that is generally available to the vast majority of individual investors.

In any successful business, relationships matter. Who you know and who you have worked with are almost foundational requisites in the world of VC. For the handful of venture firms that have established brands or sector leadership track records, opportunities arrive from a vast matrix of relationships with peer venture investors, serial entrepreneurs, attorneys, consultants, investment bankers, and service providers.[8]

Many venture capitalists invest a lot of time and energy in building relationships with government and economic development professionals, like Marsha Lyttle, who runs the Michigan Small Business and Technology Development Center (MI-SBTDC) at Kettering University in Flint, Michigan. Lyttle and Senior Growth Business Consultant Harry Blecker offer area entrepreneurs in the early stages of business development the FastTrac NewVenture program (http://fasttrac.org). This eight-week intensive course was developed by the Kauffman Foundation to not only help fledgling business owners uncover the answers they seek, but to also help them determine the right questions to ask. Programs such as this often uncover brilliant ideas that need to be directed toward the appropriate source of investment.

Business plan competitions, venture forums, and incubators like Ann Arbor SPARK (www.annarborusa.org/start-here) and Y-Combinator (http://ycombinator.com) are also fertile fishing grounds. Many successful VCs return to their alma maters to plug into the university's technology transfer offices and related corporate R&D facilities.

Relationships also come into play when it comes to putting together some of the larger deals that require a greater amount of capital investment than any single VC is comfortable or capable of providing. In these cases, several firms will do a share of the underwriting of the investment. A good example of this occurred in the third quarter of 2012 when Box, Inc. called for funding. The Los Altos, California, firm provides a secure content sharing platform. The $125,000,000 lift was spread across several VC firms including Bessemer Venture Partners, Draper Fisher Jurvetson International Inc, General Atlantic LLC, New Enterprise Associates, Inc., SAP Ventures, and Scale Venture Partners.

Alternatives to Traditional Venture Capital Funds

One of the reasons to look for alternatives to venture capital funds is the problem of the traditional VC model. The accredited investor status qualifications and minimum fund investment size requirements have been roadblocks for non-accredited investors. In addition, the traditional length of time to see a liquidity event has become problematic due to the continued economic malaise and a rapidly changing investment climate. Some VCs are beginning to doubt that many of their portfolio companies will ever see a return on investment. Those who reached an exit stage have either failed to reach the required milestones for profitability, or the return on investment has been lower than expected or required. Many VCs are shifting their focus to later-stage investments, leaving entrepreneurs and start-ups looking for alternative financing options.

Sweat Equity

It almost always begins with some form of sweat equity—a party's contribution to a project in the form of effort, as opposed to financial equity, which is credited as a contribution in the form of capital. In a partnership, some partners may contribute to the firm only capital and others only sweat equity. Similarly, in a start-up company formed as a corporation, employees may receive stock or stock options, thus becoming part owners of the firm, in return for their services or for accepting salaries below their respective market values.

There are obviously no sweat equity funds for VC investors to invest in; instead, there are individual investment opportunities where the individual's particular skill set and/or set of relationships can be negotiated for equity participation in a start-up company.

Angel Investment Opportunities

Whether known as an angel investor, a business angel, or an informal investor, an angel in the investing world is an affluent individual who typically provides up to $50,000 in capital for a business start-up, usually in exchange for convertible debt or ownership equity. An increasing number of angel investors organize themselves into angel groups or angel networks to share research and pool their investment capital. These funds average up to $250,000 per investment.

Because of the strict requirements venture capitalists have for potential investments, many entrepreneurs seek seed funding from angel investors, who may be more willing to invest in highly speculative opportunities, or may have a prior relationship with the entrepreneur.

Furthermore, many venture capital firms will only seriously evaluate an investment in a start-up company otherwise unknown to them, if the company can prove at least some of its claims about the technology and/or market potential for its product or services. To achieve this, or even just to avoid the dilutive effects of receiving funding before such claims are proven, many start-ups seek to self-finance sweat equity until they reach a point where they can credibly approach outside capital providers such as venture capitalists or angel investors. This practice is called *bootstrapping*.

There has been some debate since the year 2000 dot-com bust that a "funding gap" has developed between the friends and family investments (up to $250,000) and the amounts that most very early-stage VC funds (most often today referred to as Angel Funds of Micro-VC Funds) prefer to invest—between $500,000 and $2 million. This funding gap may be accentuated by the fact that some successful VC funds have been drawn to raise ever-larger funds, requiring them to search for correspondingly larger investment opportunities. This gap between sweat equity and seed funding is often filled by angel investors and funds who specialize in investments in start-up companies from the range of $250,000 to $1 million. The National Venture Capital Association estimates that the latter now invest an astounding $30 billion a year in the United States in contrast to the $20 billion a year invested by organized venture capital funds.

In September of 2011, New York-based AngelSoft, a platform that connects entrepreneurs with hundreds of angel investor groups around the world, announced it was rebranding and relaunching as a new service called Gust.com. Gust (http://gust.com/) is an investor relations platform that matches entrepreneurs to investors, while also providing search and filtering tools for investors that allow them to narrowly target start-ups that match their interests.

AngelSoft was founded in 2004 by New York investor David Rose. It was used by many investors to manage deal flow and for collaboration purposes. There were over 150 venture capital funds and 35,000 angels involved with

AngelSoft. Almost all of them transitioned to the new service and joined with over 50 organizations endorsing Gust. These included the Angel Capital Association, the National Association of Seed and Venture Funds, the Community Development Venture Capital Alliance, the World Business Angel Association, Microsoft BizSpark, the Young Entrepreneur Council, and the Start-Up America Partnership.[9]

Gust.com lists more than 1,000 active Angel Funds such as Tech Coast Angels, Central Texas Angel Network, Launchpad Venture Group, Golden Seeds, Investors Circle, Sand Hill Angels, Alliance of Angels, ATIF, Common Angels, Desert Angels, Atlanta Technology Angels, Y Combinator, 500 Start-ups, and First Round Capital. The funds review and invest in a number of industry sectors including technology, biotech, consumer products, Internet, IT, life science, clean-tech, and so on.

Accredited investors, both institutional and HNWI alike, are able to invest in these funds directly, and the VC fund managers who have the right to waive LP investment minimums, oftentimes do so for as little as $100,000.

Crowdfunding

Crowdfunding, also known alternately as crowd financing, equity crowdfunding, or hyper funding, describes the collective effort of individuals who network and pool their resources, usually via the Internet, to support efforts initiated by other people or organizations. Crowdfunding is used in support of a wide variety of activities, including disaster relief, citizen journalism, support of artists by fans, political campaigns, start-up company funding, movie or free software development, and scientific research.

Crowdfunding can also refer to the funding of a company by selling small amounts of equity to many investors. This form of crowdfunding has recently received attention from policy makers in the United States with direct mention in the JOBS Act: legislation that allows for a wider pool of small investors with fewer restrictions. The act was signed into law by President Obama on April 5, 2012. The U.S. Securities and Exchange Commission has been given approximately 270 days to set forth specific rules and guidelines that enact this legislation, while also ensuring the protection of investors.

A few examples of crowdfunding hoping to evolve into fully-fledged alternative funding sources include Kickstarter (www.kickstarter.com), RocketHub (www.rockethub.com), PetriDish (www.petridish.org), Indiegogo (www.indiegogo.com), and Microryza (www.microryza.com).

All of these investment options are currently available to accredited HNWIs and the investment size minimums are in many cases around $5,000. Extremely important to the VC financing community is the pending SEC clarification of the rules and guidelines that will govern the JOBS Act, not the least of which is the definition of *accredited investor*, which may have a significant impact as to whether individual retirement accounts may be used for these investments. If this occurs as expected, the availability of VC investing options to the general population will increase dramatically. In several instances, many of the established private equity and traditional VC funds are preparing adapted investment vehicles for investment by a redefined accredited investor population, estimated to exceed $5 trillion.

Stock and Warrant Off-Balance Sheet Research and Development (SWORD)

Warrants are investment securities that give the holder the right, but not the obligation, to buy a common share of stock directly from the company at a fixed price for a pre-defined time period. They are typically included as a sweetener for an equity or debt issue. Investors like warrants because they enable additional participation in the company's growth. Companies include warrants in equity or debt issues because they can bring down the cost of financing and provide assurance of additional capital if the stock does well.

SWORD financing is a financing option developed to help a biotechnology company access capital, which could be used to finance new or ongoing research and development projects by establishing a separate entity. The financing received through outside investors gives the biotechnology company the needed capital in exchange for giving the investors partial rights to the outcomes of the R&D projects they are funding.

The downside is that VCs are wary of investing in some R&D plays. A good example is a company with a new drug that is only in Phase I clinical studies. The three phases of clinical studies required for a drug to pass muster with the FDA and make it to market is typically a seven-and-a-half year process that costs an average of $325 million, with no revenue and no guarantee of ever seeing any kind of return.[10] This is a gamble which few VCs are willing to take.

SWORD special purpose investment vehicles are usually underwritten by the sponsoring corporation or their investment bank and investors include both institutions and accredited HNWIs.

Secondary Investing

The venture capital asset class is illiquid and is intended to be a long-term investment for buy-and-hold investors. The secondary market involves buying and selling of pre-existing investor (LP) commitments to venture capital including the remaining unfunded commitments to the funds.

As of 2009, it is estimated that several dedicated firms and institutional investors have made a reported $30 billion of capital available for purchase of LP interests and the purchase of existing portfolios. Vehicles for these transactions include structured joint ventures that are usually set up to transfer ownership, either over a period of time or upon meeting negotiated benchmarks. Vehicles for purchase of existing portfolios allow VCs to sell investments that have either exceeded their anticipated life or have failed to perform up to the VCs' expectations.

Secondary transaction purchasers are most often dedicated secondary funds and fund of funds that very often include secondary purchases as part of their investment strategies. Given the lack of liquidity and marketability and desire by the seller to dispose, in many instances secondary buyers are able to complete purchases at significant discounts to the underlying net asset values. Given the attractiveness of this investment option and the size of this market, currently estimated at approximately 5 percent of annual venture capital activity, secondary exchanges are appearing for secondary opportunities of all sizes, including VC portfolios and individual funds and investments.

Silver Lake Partners (www.silverlake.com) is a specialist firm focused on private technology company investments. On December 6, 2011, the firm's managing partner and managing director, Egon Durban, appeared in a breakout discussion with Andreesen-Horowitz GP John O'Farrell at the Financing Innovation seminar held at the Stanford Graduate School of Business. The most important points that came out of the discussion on private secondary markets were the substantial annual expenses incurred by a public company, which are specifically due to compliance issues under the Sarbanes-Oxley regulations. As a result, many companies are choosing to stay private longer.

The secondary market prior to an IPO serves to facilitate transactions between sophisticated buyers and sellers. It allows the GP to have a backup exit plan, but it also allows him to confidently commit the time and resources needed to help the slower-developing founder build for the long term.

Vulture Capital or Activist Funds

Investopedia.com defines a *vulture capitalist* in two ways. The first is a slang word for a venture capitalist that deprives an inventor of control over his or her own innovations and most of the money the inventor should have made from the invention. The second definition is much less derogatory and is becoming much more common in today's economy. It is a venture capitalist who invests in floundering firms in the hopes that the firms will turn around.

When a company files for bankruptcy, there can be extenuating circumstances that do not reflect the real value of the firm. Vulture capitalists do their due diligence and try to spot companies that are in bankruptcy but have a low market cap or the potential for a strong revenue stream when it emerges from bankruptcy. Such investors will buy a major interest in the distressed firm before new shares are issued with a plan to make a large return on investment when the firm returns to profitability.

Some more famous names who have utilized this method of wealth accumulation and the accompanying notoriety include, fairly or not, Mitt Romney, George Soros, Carl Ichan, and Sam Zell.

These activist investments are usually larger in scope and take place by established funds where the LPs are institutions and accredited investors.

Government-Sponsored VC

The Small Business Act of 1958 created the Small Business Administration (SBA) and allowed the creation of Small Business Investment Companies (SBIC), which are U.S. government agencies that provide support to entrepreneurs and small businesses. The mission of the SBA is "to maintain and strengthen the nation's economy by enabling the establishment and viability of small businesses and by assisting in the economic recovery of communities after disasters." The agency's activities are summarized as the "3 Cs" of capital, contracts, and counseling.

The SBA does not directly provide cash to the SBICs. Instead, the SBA guarantees loans that the SBICs take out in order to boost the amount of capital they are able to provide to businesses. SBA loans are made through banks, credit unions, and other lenders who partner with the SBA.

Regulations also limit an SBIC to only invest in a business with a tangible net worth of less than $18 million and an average $6 million in net income over the two years prior to the investment. Because they have capital guaranteed by the federal government, SBICs are less risk averse than a typical venture capital firm; however, they also tend to primarily focus on companies that are mature enough to make current interest payments on the investment, excluding most early-stage companies.

Examples here mainly include VC funds such as Alpine Investors (www.alpine-investors.com) in San Francisco; Triangle Capital Corporation's (www.tcap.com) Triangle Mezzanine Fund out of Raleigh, North Carolina; and Tampa-based KLH Capital (www.klhcapital.com), where the LPs are accredited investors.

Fund of Funds

A *fund of funds* (FoF) is known as an intermediary. It facilitates interactions between LPs and GPs by raising capital from the LPs and investing in a portfolio of both private equity and venture capital funds. Since access to private equity funds is not equal to all and performance differs across different managers, the FoF vehicle solves a problem facing both large and small investors. The larger investors, like public pension funds, can assess their capital allocation across a spectrum of smaller funds and diversify their risk. The smaller investor gains the advantages offered by a mutual fund for their private equity investment. FoFs provide monitoring services and typically charge a management fee of 1 percent. It is also customary that they share a percentage of the gains, which is usually 5 percent.[11]

FoFs are categorized by region, such as United States or Asia or Europe, and then by subasset classes. The subasset classes identify the focus or specialization of the FoF, for example venture capital, buyout, distressed, secondary markets, and so forth. Some of the largest FoFs include:

- Goldman Sachs Asset Management, USA—$33.9 billion in assets under management (AUM)
- HarborVest Partners, LLC, USA—$31.2 billion AUM
- Credit Suisse Asset Management, LLC, USA—$30.7 billion AUM
- Pantheon Ventures, Ltd, UK—$22 billion AUM
- Adams Street Partners, LLC, USA—$18.4 billion AUM
- And of course, I would be remiss if I did not mention our own GCA Emerging Markets Multi-Manager Portfolio, a $300 million private equity fund targeting 10 pre-identified SME-sized emerging and frontier market funds.

For the investor, the fund of funds offers several attractive features. It is an efficient mechanism to access various asset classes and venture funds, creating a fairly complex matrix of relatively small investments, which provides layers of risk diversification. It often allows access to high-performance managers, especially in some of the elite venture capital funds, and knowledge of emerging or next generation manager funds with potential for high performance and growth. The diversification factor also allows the investor to take advantage of trends and opportunities that arise naturally due to the ebb and flow of the economy, such as distressed real estate, sector-focused funds, turn-around funds, or foreign funds. The investor also benefits from specialized expertise in the FoF to research, track, and monitor industry trends, identify leading funds, stay abreast of GP-LP investment terms, and build relationships with key managers. For the institutional manager in particular, the FoF is a cost-effective investment solution because the due diligence, negotiations, and post-investment portfolio management is outsourced to the FoF managers.[12]

Investing in a fund of funds may achieve greater diversification. According to modern portfolio theory, the benefit of diversification can be the reduction of volatility while maintaining average returns. However, this is countered by the increased fees paid on both the FoF level, and of the underlying investment fund.

FoFs are today primarily reserved for institutional and accredited LPs, but they may soon become an attractive investment to the general population, once the SEC rules and guidelines governing the JOBS ACT are clarified.

Company Stock Options

Perhaps one of the best venture capital investments that the small investor can make is choosing the right company to work with. The value of the options associated with a successful company can outstrip the return on any single venture capital investment you are likely to make, even if you are successful.

An example, albeit an extreme case, was a friend of mine who became an early recipient of AOL stock options in 1983. He received just one-year options with a nominal value of $10,000. AOL is one of the most prolific stock splitters in history, which, over several years, generated many millions of dollars in returns to my friend. Although not an everyday occurrence, we all hear and read about Microsoft, Apple, Facebook, and Google employees who have made fortunes holding early-stage company stock options.

As shown in this chapter, there is a vast array of both traditional and nontraditional nonlisted VC investment options that are available primarily to accredited LPs. The right investment choice(s) and percentage allocations to the sector are largely dependent on the investor's risk profile, investment objectives, and investable funds, which will be discussed in greater detail in the following chapters.

Chapter Six

Investment Options—Listed

For the vast majority of investors, there is a perception that there is no tradable private equity market; however, there is a growing listed market available for buyers and sellers of private equity assets. Driven by strong demand for private equity exposure, a significant amount of capital has been committed to listed investment products for investors looking to increase and diversify their private equity exposure.

—Lou Gerken

MANY PRIVATE EQUITY (PE) fund investors would like to include market-listed PE or VC (PE) investments as part of their diversified portfolio of alternative assets. The major portfolio benefit beyond the obvious liquidity available from listed investments is that listed PE investments will have the added benefit of shortening the J-curve impact of traditional private equity investing. In lay terms, this translates into the need to first plant the seeds of investments (year one to year three, using historical averages), where the investment is not yet producing tangible returns, before you can harvest the investment returns (years four through seven). This seven-year period is referred to as the J-curve period. Moreover, as private equity investors can never with certainty predict that the current investment climate will prevail over their investments J-curve period (in some cases as short as six-months in the pre-2000 tech boom, or in other cases greater than 10 years), this added investment liquidity flexibility is a real plus in PE portfolio construction and diversification.

Finally, this public option becomes even more popular during periods of protracted sluggishness in the overall economy and resulting weakness of IPO markets. This has influenced the growth in interest in the public PE options, due to the need for PE investors at large to meet the varying liquidity needs.

What follows is a review of the listed invested options, both direct and indirect, available to PE investors.

Private Equity Exchanges

The venture capital asset class is illiquid and is intended to be a long-term investment for buy-and-hold investors. As discussed in Chapter 5, the secondary market involves buying and selling of pre-existing investor (LP) commitments to PE, including the remaining unfunded commitments to the funds. A natural evolution of the secondary PE market has been the development of private equity exchanges, which de facto provide a hybrid vehicle allowing PE investors liquidity for an otherwise illiquid asset class. Select examples of these PE exchanges platforms include the Private Equity Exchange, also known as PEQX (www.peqx.com), the Private Equity Secondary Market Liquidity Solutions, also known as NYPPEX (www.nyppex.com), SharesPost (https://welcome.sharespost.com), and SecondMarket (www.secondmarket.com).

The Private Equity Exchange is an electronic secondary market for accredited investors to buy and sell restricted shares. PEQX provides venture fund managers, family office managers, and accredited individuals a venue to rebalance their restricted share portfolios of private companies and limited partnerships.

NYPPEX provides a wide variety of liquidity solutions for interests in private funds, special purpose vehicles, trusts, and so on (e.g., buyout, venture, funds of funds, distressed debt, leveraged loans, real estate, natural resources, hedge funds, etc.), unregistered securities in private companies and their respective derivative instruments. Their core services are advisory, qualified matching services (under IRS Code 1.7704), transfer administration, block trading, and market data.

SharesPost is changing the way companies, investors, and shareholders will transact in the pre-IPO economy. Founded in 2009, SharesPost is the online platform that efficiently connects forward-thinking investors with late-stage venture-backed companies and their shareholders. They are building a market where the leading private growth companies can satisfy their shareholders' desire for liquidity without sacrificing control. They have an extensive online network of private company investors and a broad offering of independent, third-party research. It's all designed to make the process of managing secondary liquidity and raising primary capital easier and more transparent than ever before.

SecondMarket (formerly Restricted Stock Partners) is an online marketplace for buying and selling illiquid assets, including auction-rate securities, bankruptcy claims, limited partnership interests, private company stock, restricted securities in public companies, structured products, and whole loans. Its participants include global financial institutions, hedge funds, private equity firms, mutual funds, corporations, and other institutional and accredited investors. SecondMarket claims it is the world's biggest broker of venture-backed private-company stock by the value of shares traded.

In addition, several independent broker-dealers provide informal exchanges via aggregation of PE investment positions.

The size of this market, currently estimated at more than 5 percent of annual PE investment activity, makes this an attractive investment option for investors to purchase PE interests, oftentimes at a substantial discount to the accounted net asset value of the investments.

PIPEs—Private Investments in Public Equities

PIPEs are private investments in public equities. These privately structured and negotiated private placement investments in listed companies or privately-held businesses are typically offered by way of PE-related funds to accredited investors.

PIPE transactions come in many different configurations. They may involve the sale of common stock at a fixed or variable price and may include fixed-price warrants or resettable or variable-priced warrants. They may be comprised of convertible preferred stock, convertible debentures, warrants, or other equity or equity-like securities of an already-public company. They may be a change-of-control transaction or a venture-style private placement for an already-public company.

Advantages of a PIPE transaction for the recipient company include lower transaction expenses, discretion regarding public disclosure of the sale before definitive purchase commitments are made, and a quick closing, usually within 7 to 10 days. The PIPE investor benefits oftentimes by receiving a favorable price and/or terms relative to the current market price and having freely tradable securities (assuming they are registered) once the SEC certifies the resale registration.

A further advantage of PIPEs is that they are very often coupled to a value-add material event that is to transpire in a company, such as a pending merger or acquisition, a new product announcement, or new discovery. This is structured to favorably impact investor perception of the company's value as an ongoing concern.

A competitive alternative to PIPEs, a secondary offering by a public company, would likely entail underwriting fees of greater than 3 percent, take more than 90–120 days to complete (if completed), involve a full cycle of SEC securities registration, be dilutive to current shareholders (around 15 percent), and be priced with uncertainty given that pricing would be dependent on what the prevailing markets dictate 90–120 days in the future.

Besides a negotiated discount in price to investors (around 15 percent), other disadvantages to the recipient company include negotiated non-"black-out" periods during registration where PIPE investors are not restricted prior to selling their outstanding stock at a discount.

In the past, PIPEs have been confused with death spiral transactions and equity lines of credit. The term *death spiral* refers to a privately placed convertible security that has a floating conversion ratio, without a "floor." The conversion ratio of the security adjusts based upon the market price of the company's securities at some point in the future, usually at the time of conversion. Death spirals typically reset or adjust downward, protecting the investor, and not upward to protect the company. Unlike properly aligned PIPEs, these transactions can result in ongoing and substantial dilution.

The SEC's enforcement division has brought a number of actions against hedge funds and other investors in PIPE transactions that traded in advance of the public announcement of the transaction, while in possession of material non-public information (MNPI), or that engaged in manipulative trading practices in connection with PIPE transactions.[1]

A variation of the standard PIPE is the registered direct deal. This involves shares that are already registered with the Securities and Exchange Commission. The issuer completes the regulatory paperwork early through a shelf registration and has up to three years after to issue the shares, allowing a quick and quiet transaction when the market conditions are right. The issue must still be approved by the company's board of directors just as they would approve any secondary offering; but a registered direct offering is often only made to a small, prequalified group of investors and brokered bilaterally by an investment bank rather than an underwriter.[2]

In fact, the most renowned PIPE investor is Warren Buffett. Virtually every investment that Berkshire Hathaway has negotiated has been by way of a PIPE with management of a listed company. Recall the period immediately following the 2008 financial crisis, when Mr. Buffet negotiated very sizeable PIPE investments with both Goldman Sachs and Bank of America, which in both cases generated outsized returns—a vulture capitalist or just a very savvy investor?[3]

Since its inception in 1999, Silver Lake Partners (www .silverlake.com), a leading PE fund, has made investments through leveraged buyout transactions, minority growth investments, and PIPE investments. It has most recently renegotiated the acquisition of Dell Computers in a public-to-private PIPE transaction.

I recall during the immediate aftermath of the 2000 tech bubble burst when many traditional venture funds hit the reset button to focus their investment activities on PIPE investments in small-cap and micro-cap listed companies, where they could invest at significant discounts to prices already depressed by prevailing market conditions.

Examples of listed and active PIPE investors include Berkshire Hathaway, Blackstone, Carlyle, Fortress, KKR, Apollo, Blackrock, Franklin Resources, and Legg Mason. Noted examples of listed pure-play PIPE funds are ALPS Red Rock (LPEFX) and Catalyst Listed (LPEAX). Of note, as well, is that several nonlisted VC and PE funds will include, as part of their respective investment strategies, the option to make PIPE investments as market opportunities may warrant.

Corporate Venture Capital (CVC)

As VC investment periodically falls, corporations see a chance to fill the gap. This indicates the growing dynamic of cash rich corporations providing more capital, their willingness to lead rounds, and their ability to provide value-added support for start-ups at a time when traditional VC is declining. About 10.9 percent of all VC dollars going to start-ups in the first half of 2013 came from corporations. This compares with 6.1 percent in 2009. According to data from the NVCA, corporations put $1.38 billion into U.S. start-ups in the first half of 2013, the strongest year since 2008.

As Nino Marakovic, CEO of SAP Ventures says, "For corporations, there is pressure to grow and VC is a very natural arrow in the quiver of tools for corporates that are interested in innovation and growth."

Corporate venture capital funding is similar to but distinctly different from regular venture capital. VC firms are usually funded by institutional investors who serve as limited partners (LP) and seek to privately finance, fund, and often manage private companies for a finite period of time before seeking liquidity from an exit event.

Corporate VC funding is financing that is provided by typically larger corporations that may be looking to expand market share or seeking to gain competitive or technical insight. CVC investing may also be driven solely by financial return objectives that are unrelated to the organization's current strategy. CVC investing typically occurs through investing in external or affiliated business entities. Notable listed companies that offer corporate venture capital programs include SAP Ventures (www.sapventures.com), Comcast (corporate.comcast.com), Adobe (adobe.com), Amgen (amgen.com), IBM (www.ibm.com/midmarket/us /en/venturedevelopment), Google (googleventures.com), Johnson & Johnson (jjdevcorp.com), and The Walt Disney Company (steamboatvc.com).

Each company has its own unique requirements as to what business to invest in and how much. To explain corporate venture capital funding even further, let's take a look at Google and The Walt Disney Company.

When you visit the Google Ventures site, you are greeted with this statement:

> A Radically Different Kind of Venture Fund—
>
> Our hands-on teams work with portfolio companies full-time on design, recruiting, marketing, and engineering. Startup Lab is a dedicated facility and educational program where companies can meet, learn, work, and share. We invest hundreds of millions of dollars each year in entrepreneurs with a healthy disregard for the impossible.

Google Ventures invests in companies at any stage including Seed, Series A/B, and/or Growth. Investments are made to render a financial return and offer several resources to make sure that the companies they invest in succeed. The areas in which they focus their investments include gaming, mobile, life science, and consumer Internet.

Steamboat Ventures is the investing arm of The Walt Disney Company. Its name is derived from the "Steamboat Willie" production, in which Mickey Mouse first debuted.

Our mission at Steamboat Ventures is to help young companies successfully face the challenges of becoming leaders in their markets. We invest in early through growth stage companies that are pursuing opportunities at the intersection of technology, media, and consumer sectors.

This corporate venture capital firm offers funding to companies in all stages and will invest $2–$15 million in a single firm with a maximum investment of $20 million. In order for a company to receive funding, it is required that it have a Steamboat Ventures team member present on the company's board or grant observation rights.[4]

CVCs can provide an interesting option for the VC investor to access the asset class via large, listed, and well capitalized companies. It is important to note that these business units are not pure-play VC investing as they are one of many business lines within the parent organization.

Listed Spin-Offs

Spin-offs are the offspring of established companies. You take the division and turn it into a free-standing public entity. Bristol-Myers Squibb (www.bms.com) spawned Zimmer (www.zimmer.com), a maker of artificial joints, and Tyco (www.tyco.com), a conglomerate, sired ADT (www.adt.com), a maker of security systems. In many cases, the spin-offs have much better investment performance than their prior parent company. So far in 2013, there have been 11 big American spin-offs, a number that has steadily inched up in recent years, according to Spin-Off Advisors, a consultancy firm.

News Corp. spun off its publishing division, which includes the *Wall Street Journal*, *The Sun*, and *The Times* of London, on June 28, 2013.[5] Time Warner is preparing to jettison its magazine business, which includes *Time*.[6] Investors like spin-offs because they prefer focused companies to diversified ones. They also offer tasty investment returns. *Forbes* calculates that American companies have completed 80 spin-offs worth at least $500 million each between 2002 and 2012. The parent companies or "spinners" have delivered a return of 35 percent compared with 22 percent for the S&P

500. The spin-offs have delivered a return of 70 percent. Returns for firms in the Bloomberg Spin-Off Index have been 45 percent+ YTD compared with 18 percent +/− for the S&P 500 as of September 9, 2013. While not a traditional PE investment option, the listed spin-offs do merit review by PE investors for inclusion in their diversified PE portfolios.

Listed Venture Capital Funds

Listed venture capital funds have their shares traded publicly in the over-the-counter (OTC) market. This differs greatly from the vast majority of traditional PE and VC firms, which are closely held corporate or limited partnership entities. Publicly traded funds are usually entities that were created under the auspices of either the Small Business Investment Companies (SBIC) or the Business Development Companies (BDC). A listing of these entities can be found at www.tickerspy.com/index/Business-Development-Company-(BDC)-Stocks. The following are two notable examples.

Firsthand Technology Value Fund, Inc. (www.firsthandtvf.com) is a publicly traded closed-end mutual fund with investments in the solar, advanced materials, telecommunications, and semiconductor industries. Firsthand was founded in 1994 by Kevin Landis, who was born and raised in Silicon Valley and has more than 25 years of experience in technology and investment management. His team has been responsible for over $150 million of investments in more than 25 private companies over the past dozen years.

Sector funds enable you to gain exposure to a sector without having to research hundreds of individual stocks. This advantage, however, must be weighed carefully against the risks associated with sector investing. They are, by their very nature, more risky investments than their more diversified counterparts. They are nondiversified and concentrate only in their specific sector.

The Firsthand Technology Value Fund invests solely in high-tech companies, both domestic and foreign, that specialize in a wide range of industries including semiconductors, e-commerce, communications, networking, security, and software. Most of their portfolio is not comprised of household names, but they are the companies that actually produce the vital components that go into the popular laptops, smartphones, tablets, and other consumer electronics with which we're all familiar. They make the sensors, LCDs, and microprocessors that make the latest gadgets run and, more importantly, they own the valuable intellectual property.

Capital Southwest Corporation (www.capitalsouthwest .com) was founded in 1961 with the help of 21 banks and 8 individual investors. It was organized as a Texas corporation and licensed as a small business investment company (SBIC) with $15 million in assets. CSC provides funding for growth financing of existing businesses, management-led buyouts, acquisition financings, and recapitalizations. They look for firms led by management teams with proven records of achievement, exceptional ability, unyielding determination, and unquestionable integrity. These attributes in management seem to directly translate to enhanced value for customers, employees, and shareholders.

CSC's typical investment ranges from $10 million to $50 million of capital. They seek to invest in profitable operations with revenues approaching or above $10 million and historical growth of at least 15 percent per year and a market large enough to allow the company to achieve $100 million in revenues.

CSC focuses on companies that have competitive advantages in their respective markets or operate in industries that have barriers to entry, which may protect their market positions. Key sectors are energy services and products, industrial technologies, and specialty chemicals and products. CSC also considers exceptional opportunities that are outside its key sectors; however, new platform companies must be headquartered in the United States. Acquisition candidates for their existing portfolio companies can be located worldwide. They will not invest in start-ups, publicly traded companies, real estate developments, project finance opportunities, oil and gas exploration businesses, troubled companies, turnarounds, or companies in which significant senior management are departing.

Tradable Venture Capital Mutual Funds

Another option available to investors is the venture capital mutual fund. A venture capital mutual fund has one major difference in that it allows individual investors as well as institutions to invest in both nonlisted companies and listed small-cap or micro-cap enterprises. The funds are typically liquid investment instruments with daily net asset values (NAVs). Notable examples are Janus Venture Fund (JAVTX), ICON Opportunities Fund (ICONX), and Davis New York Venture Fund (NYVTX). Two select funds are summarized below.

Vanguard Explorer Fund Investor Shares (VEXPX) seeks to identify small U.S. companies with growth potential. Because it focuses on smaller companies, the fund tends to be more unpredictable than stock funds that focus on larger companies. The fund's use of multiple advisors with diverse strategies, and its broad exposure to almost 600 stocks, can help reduce—but not eliminate—risk that may come from investing in this often-volatile segment of the market. This fund may be considered complementary to a well-diversified, long-term portfolio. The minimum investment in this fund is $3,000 (https://personal.vanguard.com/us/funds/snapshot ?FundId=0024&FundIntExt=INT).

The Royce Pennsylvania Mutual Fund (PENNX) was founded in late 1972 and is managed by Royce & Associates, LLC. The fund seeks long-term capital appreciation. The fund invests at least 65 percent of its net assets in the equity securities of small and micro-cap companies. The fund invests in a more limited number of companies that have excellent business strengths, high internal rates of return, and low leverage. The fund distributes its dividends and capital gains, if any, annually in December (www.roycefunds .com/funds/royce-pennsylvania-mutual-fund).

These are but two examples. Online research sites like Zacks Investment Research (www.zacks.com) can help you find the fund that is tailored to you.

PE electronically traded funds (ETFs) are another investment option. Examples include Proshares Global Listed Private (PEX), Proshares Global PE (PSP), and iShares Listed Private Equity (IPRV). These offer trading 24/7, global diversified PE portfolios based on an underlying index, and, in select cases like PSP, also trade options.

Listed PE Funds or BDCs

A business development company (BDC) is a form of publicly traded private equity in the United States that invests in small, upcoming businesses. This form of company was created by Congress in 1980 as amendments to the Investment Company Act of 1940. Publicly traded private equity firms may elect regulation as BDCs. Typically, BDCs are structured similarly to real estate investment trusts (REITs) in that the BDC structure reduces or eliminates corporate income tax. In return, REITs are required to distribute 95 percent of their income, which may be taxable to its investors.

Among the largest BDCs (by market value, excluding Apollo Investment Corp, discussed elsewhere) are American Capital Strategies (NASDAQ: ACAS), Allied Capital (NASDAQ: ALD), Ares Capital Corp. (NASDAQ: ARCC), Gladstone Investment Corp. (NASDAQ: GAIN), and Kohlberg Capital Corp. (NASDAQ: KCAP).

There are fundamentally two separate opportunities that private equity firms pursued in the public markets. These options involved a public listing of either (1) a private equity firm (the management company), which provides shareholders an opportunity to gain exposure to the management fees and carried interest earned by the investment professionals and managers of the private equity firm; the most notable example of this public listing was completed by The Blackstone Group in 2007; and (2) a private equity fund or similar investment vehicle, which allows investors that would otherwise be unable to invest in a traditional private equity limited partnership to gain exposure to a portfolio of private equity investments. Examples include Blackstone (BX), Apollo Global (APO), KKR (KKR), Invesco (IVZ), and American Capital (ACAS).

Other alternatives available include LPX Europe, an index that tracks European listed PE funds, London-listed J.P. Morgan, 3i Group, HgCapital, Better Capital, SCG Capital, Electra Private Equity, and Candover Investments.

Although there had previously been certain instances of publicly traded private equity vehicles, the convergence of private equity and the public equity markets attracted significantly greater attention when several of the largest private equity firms listed herein pursued various options through the public markets. Taking private equity firms and private equity funds public appeared an unusual move since private equity funds often buy public companies listed on the exchange and then take them private. Private equity firms are rarely subject to the quarterly reporting requirements of the public markets, and they tout this independence to prospective sellers as a key advantage of going private.[7]

After years of trading at large discounts to their portfolio valuations—about 30 percent since the 2008 financial crisis, primarily due to the underlying portfolios being extremely illiquid, the overall discount is currently at a healthier and more normal 15 percent, reflecting the improved market, and a change in investment strategies, where PE funds have responded to pressure to narrow discounts and started to return more money to shareholders and introduce share buybacks. That said, there is no reason why this group could not trade at a premium to NAV as they did before the financial crisis.

In summary, it is probably surprising even to the most sophisticated followers of the PE industry to see the breadth and depth of listed options that are increasingly available to the VC investor, both accredited and nonaccredited. And with further expected developments such as the much anticipated SEC roll-out of the JOBS ACT, it will be certain that listed PE options will play a more important role in the VC investors construction of a diversified PE portfolio—to be discussed in more detail in the chapters that follow.

Chapter Seven

Investment Process—Sourcing and Screening

_~_

Whether you're a GP, LP, or entrepreneur trying to raise capital or invest in the VC asset class, the investment process—sourcing and screening, diligence and selection, and monitoring and monetization, are basically the same discipline. Here we look through the lens of the LP.

—Lou Gerken

IN THE 1970 MOVIE CATCH 22, there is a great scene between "Doc" Daneeka, played by veteran character actor Jack Gilford, and Captain John Yossarian, played by Alan Arkin.

Yossarian is a World War II bomber pilot who has been forced to fly 50 percent more missions than he was told he would have to fly before being rotated back to the States. He is trying to get "Doc," the unit flight surgeon, to ground him. That way, he figures, he can't be forced to fly anymore. It sounds like a good plan; but, as Doc explains, there's a catch.

Yossarian:	So in order to be grounded, I've *got* to be crazy. And I *must* be crazy to keep flying. But if I *ask* to be grounded, that means I'm *not* crazy anymore and I *have* to keep flying.
Doc:	You got it. That's Catch 22.

So it is in the world of venture capital investing. The institutional investors won't invest any money unless you are a proven VC. The VC, in turn, looks for the entrepreneur who has some skin in the game and has shown he can raise enough money to prove his concept and generate some revenue. It's a classic Catch 22 situation. Nobody will give you money unless you can prove you don't need it. Further complicating the Catch 22 is the frequent complaint of entrepreneurs that they are unable to meet VCs who are willing to actually lead financing rounds, do the heavy lifting, or move quickly.

Many entrepreneurs think VCs are being unnecessarily demanding of them, but the VC does not usually ask anything of the entrepreneur that he did not have to endure while going through the institutional investor's screening process. VCs don't normally just hang out a shingle and have investors hand them bags of money, although there are exceptions once a VC has established a successful track record. They also have to go through a qualification process before entering into the limited partner–general partner (LP-GP) relationship.

As an asset class, venture capital faces enormous competition for the finite pool of investment capital that is available every year. Hedge funds have raised trillions of dollars in the aggregate while the private equity industry averages about $300 billion per year. The venture capital slice of the pie is only about a tenth of that.[1] The heydays of the 1980s and 1990s, when venture was the best action in town, are now becoming faded memories. It is imperative that today's VCs fully understand the investment criterion of their potential LPs. The name of the game now is return on investment. That starts with screening.

Sourcing and Deal Flow

The LP's screening process begins with fund sourcing, or deal flow, screening to select funds that meet the investment criteria, and diligence—the comprehensive process of investigation, reference checks, background checks, and so on. This is a process that evaluates the GP investment team's track record, relevant expertise, and investment strategy.

The first criterion that must be met is to find a VC who complements the institution's investment mandate. This may be a requirement only to invest with the established top decile or quartile performing fund managers, a requirement common with endowment fund investors. Other criteria may be investment-stage or sector-specific, or they may require investments only in biotech or environmental funds. Still others may have geographic or demographic considerations that chart the direction of their investing and define the returns they seek. These are important considerations when you consider that this VC fund partnership is going to last from 7 to 10 years in most cases. Moreover, it is of paramount importance to right-size, right-fit the fund selected to the prevailing investment climate, as there are numerous examples of brand name funds who have not returned LP capital.

Private Placement Memorandum (PPM)

When VCs are courting potential LPs, they submit a private placement memorandum (PPM), which describes the type of fund they are seeking to create. In layman's terms, a PPM is usually a lengthy document that is half marketing and half legal disclosures. It is sometimes described as "essentially a traditional business plan wrapped in legal disclaimers that are often as long as the plan itself."[2] It typically defines the fund, the investment parameters, the relationship, and usually contains many boilerplate clauses. It attempts to concisely touch upon all of the important features of the fund that would be of interest to the investor and entice him or her to enter into an LP-GP relationship.

The general partner is identified, including the organizational structure and where domiciled. That is followed by a statement about the investment objective of the fund. This is one of the initial screens used by the institutional investor because it describes in what sector the fund will be investing or where it will focus its activities.

The basic structure of the fund is then described, including such items as the anticipated size of the fund in dollars, the term of the fund in years, management fees, minimum contributions, and a description of the GP's commitment. This last item is becoming more and more important. Whereas VCs have traditionally invested about 1 percent of the total fund from their own resources (the IRS guideline for GPs meeting the capital at risk requirement), LPs are now seeking funds in which the GP has more skin in the game. It is not uncommon to see as much as 5 percent of the fund coming from the GP; thus the growing tendency of institutional investors to use a successful track record as another of the initial screens.

The PPM will describe how the investment will be drawn down (typically quarterly over a fund's five-year investment commitment period) or reinvested (where fund distributions can be reinvested by the fund GP) and whether there will be any restrictions or limitations with respect to flow of funds. The PPM will describe who determines what investments are made and how they will be executed. Allocation of profits and losses, distributions, and any other specifics describing the flow of returns from the GP back to the LP will also be addressed. Fund distributions are most often in the following sequence; first, recoupment of investment capital; second, a 6 to 8 percent preferred return to the LPs; and last, a sharing in gains, which typically breaks down to 80 percent to the LP and 20 percent to the GP.

An entire section will be devoted to the management and governance of the fund and will include clauses that define the investment period, key person events, termination or removal of the GP, transfer of LP interests, expenses, and audits.

Finally, there is a section on legal, taxation, and regulatory matters that is usually boilerplate language addressing liabilities, indemnification, and other related issues.

While it may seem pretty straightforward, this document will become the basis of serious negotiations should the institutional investor decide to move forward on entering the LP-GP relationship (the LP Agreement). For instance, expenses are broken down into two categories. The management fee (typically 2 to 2.5 percent of committed investment capital) is expected to cover such items as the GP's salaries, rent, office equipment and supplies, entertainment, and bookkeeping. The fund or the corpus is expected to cover legal fees, audit and accounting fees, liability insurance, and all portfolio-related expenses. Another recent phenomenon that is becoming an irritant to LPs is something called style drift. It has been traditional for GPs to have latitude to invest up to 10 percent of a fund in "targets of opportunity" that happen to come to their attention. Perhaps it is the result of the prolonged economic doldrums, but some GPs have been observed investing larger and larger percentages of funds into companies that have only a passing acquaintance with anything remotely resembling the investment objective of the fund. For endowment and foundation investors who are bound by charter to invest in very specific areas, this can become a serious issue.

Relationships Really Do Matter

Institutional investors see anywhere from 200 to 600 PPMs every year. How to cut through that clutter and stand out from the crowd brings us to yet another and, perhaps, the most important screen in the early stage of the investment process—relationship. The hunt for the elusive big return is indeed a two-way street, so it is natural to engage in that activity with someone you trust and with whom you have some sort of rapport. That begins with introductions at conferences and industry events, usually by mutual colleagues. Sometimes it begins with discovering mutual interests or through networking opportunities.

Getting in the door is the challenge, but the most important factor in building a long-term and profitable relationship is the integrity of performance. Past successful investment or operational experience can be a major indicator of what the LP can expect. Domain expertise is very important; however, the experienced VC fund manager is also cognizant of the importance of his or her academic, industry, and political connections, civic engagement, and volunteer involvement. Soft skills such as listening, qualitative analysis, cognitive reasoning, and public speaking are also attractive attributes, which increase perceived professionalism. All of these offer insights to the LP as to the quality of the relationship going forward and account for the GP's social capital.

Social capital in the VC arena can help a practitioner access opportunities, conduct due diligence, syndicate investments, accelerate exits, and mitigate risks.[3] Who you know really does matter just as much as what you know.

The GP's Network

The same holds true for the GP in search of the one investment that is going to make his new fund a success. On average, a typical VC firm logs 1,000 investment opportunities over the course of a year and makes only 3 or 4 investments. These opportunities arrive on the VC's desk from a myriad of sources. The countless cold pitches and business plans that come across the transom have little chance of competing against the recommended ventures that come from members of the VC's personal network.

Relationships with investment bankers, serial entrepreneurs, peer VC investors, attorneys, and other related industry insiders often lead to excellent leads on new ventures before they gain public exposure. Benchmark Capital (www.benchmark.com), for instance, was able to make a $5 million first round investment in eBay, which ended up netting them $2.5 billion. This was possible because Bruce Dunlieve, a Benchmark GP, had invested in a previous venture of eBay founder Pierre Omidyar. They knew and trusted each other.

What a VC Wants

What is a VC looking for when he sets out to find a potential venture in which to invest? According to Guy Kawasaki, founder and managing director of Garage Technology Ventures (www.garage.com), there are a few factors that can make a company appear fundable:

A compelling idea: Every entrepreneur believes her idea is compelling. The reality is that very few business plans present ideas that are unique. It is very common for investors to see multiple versions of the same idea over the course of a few months, and then again after a few years. What makes an idea compelling to an investor is something that shows a clear depth of understanding of a big problem or opportunity, and offers an elegant solution. Nothing is more compelling to venture capitalists than a company that may have a big impact on the world.

Team: You may have a great idea, but if you don't have a strong core team, investors won't be willing to bet on your company. The founders must have the credibility to launch the company and attract the world-class talent that is needed to fill the gaps.

Market opportunity: If you are focused on a product/market opportunity that is not technology-based, you probably should not be pursuing venture capital—there are different private equity sources for nontechnology businesses. Venture capital is focused on businesses that gain a competitive edge and generate rapid growth through technological and other advantages. It is about how much value you can create.

Technology: What is it about your technology that makes it so great? The correct answer is that there are plenty of customers with plenty of money who desperately want or need it.

Competitive advantage: Every interesting business has real competition. Competition is not just about direct competitors. It includes alternatives, "good enough" solutions, and the status quo. You need to convince investors that you have advantages that address all of these forms of competition, and that you can sustain these advantages over several years.

Financial projections: If the idea of developing credible financial projections makes you wince or wail, or if you think it's a meaningless exercise, you are not an entrepreneur, and you shouldn't ask investors for money. Your projections demonstrate that you understand the finance and economics of your business. They should tell your story in numbers—what drives your growth, what drives your profit, and how will your company evolve over the next several years.

Validation: Probably the most important factor influencing investors is validation. Do you have customers and cash flow? Is your deal clean, or are their lawsuits waiting in the wings for the first whiff of money? The more credibility and customer traction you have, the more likely investors are going to be interested.[4]

Searching High and Low

Serial entrepreneurs make the best sources for leads on potential winning investments. They have been through the process and can spot a well-thought-out and critically appraised business idea. They recognize the challenges and can identify someone who has the ability to assemble a winning team. Angel investors and peer VCs with whom there is a trusted relationship can also be good sources for an introduction.

Attending industry conferences and seminars provides the VC with access to professionals in government, economic development, and nonprofit agencies. These relationships provide insights into the investment climate and may expose targets of opportunity in certain geographic areas. A great example of this is the palette of economic incentives being assembled by the State of Michigan, county and local governments, and private funding organizations like Invest Detroit (investdetroit.com) to begin the economic rebuilding of Detroit following its bankruptcy.

It is no accident that Sand Hill Road is right next to the campus of Stanford University. From the very beginning, with the founding of ARDC by Harvard professor Georges Doriot and MIT president Karl Compton, there has been a symbiotic relationship between VCs and universities. One VC firm, Osage University Partners (osagepartners.com), is a venture capital fund that invests exclusively in start-ups that are commercializing university research. Their $100 million fund includes such disruptive portfolio companies as Liquid Light, Luxtera, Inc., and MC10, Inc.

Venture capitalists who spend time mining investment opportunities on university campuses are sometimes rewarded in legendary ways. In the fall of 1998, a computer science professor, Jeffrey Ullman, introduced two of his students, Sergey Brin and Larry Page, to Netscape investor Kavitark Ram Shriram while the investor was visiting Stanford University.[5] Shriram's initial $250,000 investment in Google helped land him on the *Forbes* magazine list of the 400 Richest People in America with a net worth in excess of $1.75 billion.[6]

Other avenues for deal sourcing include corporate research and development labs, a particularly fertile source of biotech investments. Pitch events at venture conferences and trade fairs provide opportunities for VCs to walk the aisles and assess industry trends, meet with technical thought leaders, and appear on panels where they have an opportunity to educate entrepreneurs on the VC process. Incubators like TechStars (www.techstars.com) and Y Combinator (ycombinator.com) develop young entrepreneurs and establish meaningful relationships with mentors and investors.

It Starts at "Hello . . ."

There is an old adage that goes, "Nothing happens until somebody sells something." This is most apropos in the world of venture capital when it comes to deal sourcing. The Catch 22 is that it is the aura of a VC firm's brand, which is a by-product of its history of performance, which in turn determines the quality of the opportunities it attracts. And that depends solely on how well the GP sells his firm's deal flow to the LP.

The GP can only be successful by finding entrepreneurs who have something to sell. Whether you are selling a

Figure 7.1   The Investment Process

product, a service, or a cure for the world's worst disease, you are never going to be funded until you manage to get in front of a venture capitalist who cares about what you have to say and is willing to listen. That begins with an introduction. How you get the introduction is up to you, but consider this: Why would a VC put enough faith in you that he is willing to risk the LP's money to fund your venture if you do not have the determination and ingenuity to figure out a way to get an introduction? That should be the ultimate screening process.

In summary, we close with the investment process flow chart (Figure 7.1), which identifies the sourcing and screening steps covered in this chapter. The diligence and selection steps are covered in Chapter 8, with the monitoring and monetization steps covered in Chapter 9.

It is important to all investors that you do your own research, and only invest in what you understand and feel comfortable with.

Lou Gerken

Chapter Eight

Investment Process— Due Diligence and Selection

---~---

An investment in knowledge pays the best interest.

—Benjamin Franklin

IF THE SOURCING and screening portion of the investment process is likened to the initial thrill of a budding romance, this next part of the process is where the question gets asked, "Where are we going with this relationship?" Unlike romance, the ultimate goal is a liquidity event leading to an exit that causes all parties involved to feel as though their time and money has been put to good use. That "exit" could be in many different forms. The most satisfactory outcomes are usually in the form of an initial public offering (IPO) or, more likely, a merger or acquisition (M&A) with another company. Sometimes, the outcome may be a company recapitalization or another round of financing, either because of continued belief in the potential of the portfolio company or because of the need to bring in different parties with different skills or a fresher perspective. A buyout of interest on the secondary market can be a sign of the parties trying to salvage as much of the investment as they can before writing off the relationship as nonproductive, or may quite simply be a change in the LP's allocation strategy, which forces the requirement of a sale.

LP Due Diligence of the VC

Due diligence is a term used to define the process of using a certain standard of care to discover as many relevant, objective facts about the person or persons with whom you are about to enter into an agreement or transact a business arrangement. It is usually a legal requirement involving a voluntary investigation of a business or person prior to signing a contract.

For the institutional investor, this involves carefully considering every aspect of the individual (and his team) with whom you are going to be partnered for the next 7 to 10 years. Aside from a secondary sale, it is very difficult to pull out of a limited partner–general partner (LP-GP) relationship without legal cause once the deal has been consummated and the investment made.

Pension plans from government entities, private companies, or nonprofit organizations make up about 40 percent of the total available pool of committed capital available for venture capital. Financial institutions such as commercial banks, investment banks, and insurance companies provide about 18 percent. University endowments and charitable foundations make up about 17 percent, followed by high-net-worth individuals and families, who provide about 11 percent of the VC pool, either individually or through private family offices. Corporations put in another 9 percent, but lately most of that has been targeted toward biotech ventures.[1]

Whether it is an endowment fund of a university, a pension fund, or a family office managing the wealth of a high-net-worth individual, the LP has a fiduciary responsibility to protect the principal and seek out the optimum return on any investment. For most institutional investors, venture capital is a small portion of their total investment allocation (usually part of an overall 20 percent portfolio allocation to alternative assets), but it can be an important part that can provide an enormous return on investment. Historical data reveals that a minimum 5 percent portfolio allocation to VC is required to enable investors to tap into VC's efficient frontier of investment returns, which is typically 12 to 15 percent.

Dimensions of a Great GP

When an LP is evaluating a potential GP, there are several factors that consistently show up across the board. First and most important is the ability and skill in managing the investment team. It can be manifested in investment and operational experience, sector expertise, regional and political connections, and team effectiveness.

Team effectiveness is the result of clearly defined roles and responsibilities, alignment of economic incentives, and good decision-making skills. The best teams are grown over time with organizational stability, pride of performance, and clear policies for career development and succession. Good GPs have a reputation for consistency and dealing with their staffs with integrity, with respect to GP commitment percentages, incentives, independence, conflicts of interest, and promotion of outside activities. Their teams work well together through good times and bad times. There is internal trust, which manifests organizational pride and confidence.

Following team management, the GP is evaluated on his fund management skills. Does he have sourcing skills? Is he limited to a particular stage or sector? What size of fund is he comfortable managing? Does he have a good exit strategy? The structure of the proposed fund is also evaluated with respect to the governance of the fund, the costs to be borne by the fund and the management fees to be extracted, and the mechanism for tracking and effectively managing compliance issues.

Finally, the LP looks at the VC's track record with the individual partners to assess who is delivering and who is an empty suit, evaluates the history of performance with comparable funds, and, most important examines the relevance of the track record to the current fund's investment strategy and prevailing investment climate. Has his performance consistently generated returns across multiple economic cycles? What was the quality of his previous co-investors? Does he have recurring investors? What is his reputation among his peers and other industry-related professionals? Once the LP has weighed all of these factors together, the decision is usually made based upon documents called the Due Diligence Questionnaire and the Investment Recommendation Report. These reports distill reams of analyzed data into an executive summary, which covers the fund manager's background and experience, his previous results, his strengths and his weaknesses, the pros and cons of the VC firm, the reasons the fund would be a good fit for the investor's investment portfolio, the rationale for investing, and the proposed amount of the investment. From this report, the investor's board will make the final determination as to whether or not this particular GP will be a good fit given the investment mandate under which they are operating.[2]

The Truth and Nothing but the Truth

The venture capital industry historically relied upon self-reporting. As a result, there have been instances in the past where bad managers have manipulated their data, omitted less than favorable information about their performance, or just flat out lied about the ratio of their successes to their failures. There was a time when a VC with more hubris than fidelity might have gotten away with such deception. Those days are gone. Today, VCs adhere to strict and uniform industry standards and practices adopted by the National Venture Capital Association (NVCA), generally accepted accounting principles (GAAP), and the International Association of Accounting Professionals (IAAP).

The hundreds of private placement memorandums (PPMs) that land on an LP's desk every year do not just get read and filed away for future reference. Beyond the vetting resources available via VC gatekeepers, consultants, data & research firms, and placement agents, institutional investors often have had their own team of analysts comb through those documents, and they have developed databases that can be sliced, diced, and evaluated in any number of ways. Each LP has built its own database as an assessment tool. So, if it has ever crossed your mind that you can just fudge the numbers and get that big endowment to capitalize your fund—forget about it. In this business, fidelity is not just the name of a fund. It is your lifeblood. Even a whiff of any issues of veracity is a nonstarter.

Unlike any other asset class that I have observed, VC funds possess huge barriers to entry, in large part reflecting the very institutional process of raising capital from institutional investors.

Getting to the First Close

Once the VC has been deemed worthy of investment and the institutional investor has committed to investing in the fund, it is time for the "related industry professionals" or "outside service providers" to take over and formalize the LP/GP agreement. A prospective venture capitalist might think that he only needs a lawyer to draw up the agreements, but he would be very, very wrong. Venture capital is nothing if not a job creator. Besides a law firm well versed in the language and customs of the VC universe, the related industry professionals include accountants, insurance brokers, investment bankers, valuation specialists, financial services representatives, corporate restructuring specialists, executive search personnel specializing in outsourcing, CFOs, advisors, advocates, philanthropy service providers, shareholder representatives, and many more.

The objective of some of these people is to get the VC to the first close of the fund. This is the point where about 50 percent of the total fund has been raised and most of the balance has been committed. This is the time when the VC can start investing in those promising entrepreneurs who have been pitching him the greatest ideas that anyone has ever conceived. The lawyers are first up, and they draw up several documents that spell out in great detail and legalese the details of the fund and the roles and responsibilities of everyone involved in the process. These documents usually include the Limited Partnership Agreement (LPA), which has its roots in the PPM; the marketing and legal disclosures document, which the GP originally submitted to the LP during the fund sourcing effort; the subscription agreements, one for each of the LPs; the General Partner Agreement, an internal document that spells out the roles and responsibilities of the GP's team; and any side letters that may be necessary.[3]

Once all of the agreements have been executed, the attorney and GPs set the closing date of the fund. GP fund managers execute the subscription agreements and accept closing subscriptions. Wire transfers of funds are completed. There is time for a brief celebration, and then the real work begins. The entire process takes about 60 days to complete and requires the skill of an attorney who is well versed in the process.

The Limited Partnership Agreement (LPA)

The LPA is a more formal, legally binding document that spells out the control and management of the capital being invested, the size of the fund being raised, the life span of the fund, the projected dates of the first close and final close of the fund, and the distribution of the returns.[4]

The size of the fund being raised is important to the LP because it is extremely rare for an institutional investor to commit the total amount of a fund, but the fund usually must be large enough to be viable. The LP's primary concern is that the GP not try to raise a fund that strains the GP's investment or management skills. If the GP is unsuccessful in raising the projected fund by the first close milestone, most LPs want language in the LPA that disbands the fund. Another clause in the LPA spells out the percentage that the GP is supposed to invest in the fund. This shows that the GP's commitment to the fund must meet the 1 percent IRS guideline of "capital at risk," which has, since about 2009, averaged around 2.5 percent of the total fund for VCs.

On the GP's side of the LPA, the minimum and maximum contribution from each LP is spelled out. This is to limit the number of investors to a manageable group and to prevent undue influence from any single investor. LPs are also concerned about limiting the number of investors in a fund so as not to trigger the investment advisor registration requirements of the Investment Company Act of 1940. Nobody wants the complex regulatory and disclosure headaches of that particular piece of well-intentioned legislation.

A VC fund has a typical life of 10 years, and the LPA includes terms that cover whether or not that period can be extended and under what conditions. Although the LP commits the investment capital to the fund, it is usually contributed gradually over the life of the fund by way of drawdown requests made by the GP. The LPA usually calls for the investment drawdowns to take place over the first five years of the fund, followed by five years of *following on activity* leading to preparing the portfolio company for an exit. Other clauses in the LPA cover how the GP will manage the fund, the recourse the LP has for dealing with the mismanagement of the GP, transfer of LP interests via the secondary market, and a host of clauses covering the definition of transaction costs, fees, and how each is handled.

Finally, the LPA deals with how profits and losses are handled. The LP recovers their investment first, plus a 6–8 percent preferred return. After that, any remaining profits are split, 80 percent going to the LPs with the GP retaining the remaining 20 percent. Whether the limited partners split is pro rated or shared equally is usually spelled out in the LPA. The GP portion is often held in escrow for a period to cover any claw backs that may surface at the end of the fund.[5]

Subscription Agreement

The subscription agreement is an application that the general partner provides to each one of the potential limited partners, which informs the potential LPs of their suitability to participate in the investment of the partnership, the risk inherent in it, and the investor's liability, which is limited to the amount invested in the partnership. It acknowledges that the limited partners have been informed of the terms to which they will be bound once accepted into the partnership.

Best Intentions

History has shown that no matter how thorough the lawyers and accountants may be, there are some things that just can't be codified in the limited partnership agreement. Recognizing that these intangibles fell roughly into three categories—alignment of interest, governance, and transparency—the Institutional Limited Partners Association (ILPA) drafted the ILPA Private Equity Principles with the hope that they would serve as constructive talking points to help clarify the expectations and intent of both parties to the LPA. Although written for the private equity (PE) industry, institutional investors have expressed their hope that VC practitioners use them, as well. Here is just a small sample of these suggested operating principles.

Alignment of interest between LPs and GPs is best achieved when GPs' wealth creation is primarily derived from carried interest and returns generated from a substantial equity commitment to the fund, and when GPs receive a percentage of profits after LP return requirements are met. The GP should have a substantial equity interest in the fund, and it should be contributed in cash as opposed to being contributed through the waiver of management fees.

Regarding issues of *governance*, the stated investment strategy is an important dimension that LPs rely on when making a decision to commit to a fund. Most LPs commit funds within the context of a broad portfolio of investments—alternative and otherwise—and select each fund for the specific strategy and value proposition it presents. The fund's strategy must therefore be well defined and consistent. The investment purpose clause should clearly and narrowly outline the investment strategy.

Transparency calls for GPs to provide detailed financial, risk management, operational, portfolio, and transactional information regarding fund investments. This enables LPs to effectively fulfill their fiduciary duties as well as to act on proposed amendments or consents. LPs acknowledge the important responsibility they bear with higher transparency in the form of confidentiality.[6]

Now that we've seen what the GP has to go through in order to get to the point of being able to raise a fund and make investments, it should make more sense as to why the VC is so particular when it comes to selecting an entrepreneur to invest in. Let's take a look at the due diligence process from the VC's perspective.

What Do You Have under the Hood?

It is important for you, the entrepreneur, to understand why the due diligence process is necessary. Start with the end in mind. This is a relationship that is going to last in some cases up to 10 years and, hopefully, result in a liquidity event that is going to handsomely reward all parties involved. In the intervening period, the VC is going to invest a multitude of resources in you and your venture—not just money. There's also time, sector expertise, management skills, sector relationships, operational experience, and investment exit know-how. The goal is to get you from the raw, untested neophyte with a good idea in the case of a start-up without a serial entrepreneur at the helm—where you might be now—to the revenue-generating going concern on the cusp of long-term profitability and growth. Wouldn't it be a tragedy to invest all of these resources and get to the point where a Fortune 50 company wants to acquire you and your technology for a ten-figure price tag, only to have it discovered that the intellectual property so key to your venture was appropriated from your college roommate's graduate research project? Stranger things have happened.

Let's assume integrity is your stock in trade. You have managed to gain an introduction to a VC who has expertise in your field of endeavor and has a newly-minted fund that just happens to be ready to begin investing. You've wowed him with the energy and passion of your elevator pitch, in which you have clearly and succinctly explained a sophisticated renewable energy breakthrough in a simple and straightforward manner, emphasizing the enormous and untapped profit potential in an underserved and growing market. You have successfully presented your Executive Summary and your 12-slide PowerPoint pitch deck to the VC and his partners. They are interested and want more information.[7] What is your next move?

Business Plan or Business Model?

Steve Blank is a serial entrepreneur and a consulting associate professor at Stanford University. He is widely recognized as the unofficial chronicler of Silicon Valley and an expert on the subject of high-tech startups. In the May 2013 edition of the *Harvard Business Review*, he wrote an article entitled "Why the Lean Start-Up Changes Everything." One of his observations was very telling about where we are with the traditional process of obtaining venture capital financing for a new venture today.

> According to conventional wisdom, the first thing every founder must do is create a business plan—a static document that describes the size of

an opportunity, the problem to be solved, and the solution that the new venture will provide. Typically it includes a five-year forecast for income, profits, and cash flow. A business plan is essentially a research exercise written in isolation at a desk before an entrepreneur has ever begun to build a product. The assumption is that it's possible to figure out most of the unknowns of a business in advance, before you raise money and actually execute the idea.[8]

Blank cites a recent study by Harvard Business School Senior Lecturer Shikhar Ghosh, in which it was shown that of 2,000 companies that received venture funding between 2004 and 2010, about 75 percent of them failed to have a successful exit.[9]

Blank is an evangelist for an alternative framework called the *business model canvas*, which is essentially a diagram of how a company creates value for itself, its customers, and its investors. Blank is credited with formulating the tools for the process in 2003 while teaching a course on entrepreneurship at the Haas School of Business at the University of California at Berkeley. He detailed his theory on customer development process in his book, *The Four Steps to the Epiphany* (K&S Ranch, 2003). It was further articulated by Alexander Osterwalder and Yves Pigneur in

Business Model Generation (John Wiley & Sons, 2010) and the *Lean Startup*, by Eric Ries (Random House, 2011). Finally, Blank and Bob Dorf summarized the lessons learned while developing this new paradigm in the step-by-step handbook, *The Startup Owner's Manual* (K&S Ranch, 2012).

Keep in mind that due diligence is an investigation or audit of a potential investment and refers to the care a reasonable person should take before entering into an agreement or a transaction with another party.[10] Many of the assumptions in the typical business plan are based upon well-established facts drawn from past industry experience or straightforward deductions. The financial information is usually an accounting exercise based upon those assumptions, in which a snapshot of present-day costs are projected five years into the future. In other words, they are a SWAG (Scientific-Wild-Ass-Guess); the entrepreneur's detailed leap of faith.[11] If he is right on target, or just a really good writer, the probability of success will seem high. What if his assumptions are wrong? As Brad Feld, a co-founder and managing director of the Foundry Group, says:

> The only thing that we know about financial predictions of startups is that 100 percent of them are wrong.[12]

After all that a VC has to go through to raise a fund, is it any wonder that only a handful of proposals get funded out of the thousand or so that he looks at every year?

The business model canvas provides a rationale for how the venture creates, delivers, and captures value. It is comprised of nine building blocks that cover the four main areas of any business, which are customers, offer, infrastructure, and financial viability. The nine building blocks are, in the order in which they are addressed, customer segments (CS), value propositions (VP), channels (CH), customer relationships (CR), revenue streams (RS), key resources (KR), key activities (KA), key partnerships (KP), and cost structure (CS).

This is not to say that the entrepreneur does not have to make any assumptions using the business model canvas, but the assumptions are derived from a progressive customer-centric process, not an attempt to project your start-up as a large corporation in just a few short years.

The first building block is called customer segments. Without customers, there is no point in being in business, and there is no way to generate the revenues needed to be successful. The entrepreneur defines and segments his possible customers based upon which market segment he is focusing. A company focusing on mass markets doesn't segment customers and has different value propositions, channels, and customer relationships from an entrepreneur who is focusing on a niche market. Walmart sells seasonal, casual clothing to the widest possible demographic and is classified as having a mass market CS. Juicy Couture is marketed as a high-end clothing line and is aimed at females aged 10–26 and is considered a niche CS. An example of a segmented CS would be a bank that classifies its customer base as personal, business, or high net worth. A diversified CS is Amazon.com, which uses its powerful IT infrastructure to sell products and also sells cloud computing services. Finally, there is the multi-sided CS platform. An example of this would be a manufacturer of an artificial hip whose CS would be divided between the patient who needs a new hip, the doctor who installs the new hip, the hospital where the operation takes place, the insurance company who pays for the new hip, and the regulatory agency, the FDA, who approves the new hip. Your customer segment is not just paying customers, but also includes users. That is why it is so important for the entrepreneur to carefully define who his customers are. You can have more than one CS.

The second building block is value propositions (VP). This is the bundle of products and services that create value for each of your customer segments. Your VP solves a customer's problem or satisfies a customer's needs. Typical VPs are based upon newness, price, cost reduction, risk reduction, performance, design, utility, or status. We called this the 4Ps—product, placement, price, and promotion—when I took Marketing 101 in business school.

The third building block is channels (CH). Channels are the touch points through which you are interacting with your customers. CH includes how you communicate with your customers and deliver your value proposition; CH includes raising awareness, allowing customers to purchase specific goods and services, delivering the VP to each CS, providing post-purchase customer support, and helping customers evaluate the company's VP.

Customer relationships (CR) make up the fourth building block in the business model canvas. CR describes the types of relationships a company establishes with each CS and is driven by three basic motivations: customer acquisition, customer retention, and upselling. Here, of course, CRM experts like Oracle and Salesforce.com have thrived offering products and services.

Revenue streams (RS) are the next building block. This is where the entrepreneur first tackles the numbers. If the customer segments are the heart of the business, the RS is the lifeblood. As a company owner, you must ask how much each CS would pay for the VP you are offering to them. Will the RS pricing mechanism be fixed-price, negotiations, bidding, market-dependent, volume-dependent, or part of a yield-management scheme? Will the RS result for one-time transactions or from recurring activities? What do customers currently pay for similar VP? What would they prefer to pay?

Building block six is key resources (KR). KR are the indispensible infrastructure, assets, and resources required to make the company function properly. KR can be physical, financial, intellectual, or human resources. KR can be owned, leased, or acquired from key partners. Needless to say, the advent of cloud-based infrastructure has dramatically reduced the cost of starting an IT-based business and has advanced business scalability by leaps and bounds.

Key activities (KA), the seventh building block, are the most important things the company *must* do in order to make the business model work. These are the activities that are critical for the company to be able to create, offer, and deliver the VP. They are necessary for you to reach and maintain each of your CS. They are required in order for you to generate your RS. These business milestones are a subject we will come back to later in this chapter.

The eighth building block in the business model is key partnerships (KP). This describes the network of suppliers and partners that make your business work. These partnerships allow you to optimize your efforts, maximize your results, reduce your risk, and acquire resources. Here, the right VC partner can provide extremely valuable value-add by way of relationships and know-how.

The ninth and final building block is the cost structure (CS) of your company. How much does it cost for you to create VP, maintain CR, and generate RS? Is your business cost driven or value driven? What are your fixed costs? What are your variable costs? Are there economies of scale or scope that you can use to reduce your costs?

Once you have completed a business model canvas, you have the framework for seeing the big picture of your operations and the ability to drill down by performing a SWOT analysis (internal and external strengths-weaknesses-opportunities-threats) of every one of the building blocks. Your financials will have meaning and context. You will easily be able to see areas in which you can make adjustments to possibly open new CS that you hadn't even considered or spot opportunities to strengthen or even replace key activities or partnerships. You will have a visual representation that will easily illustrate and help you define your strategy, your structure, your processes, your rewards, and your people. You will have answered a vast majority of the VC's questions before he or she even gets to ask them. That will instill confidence in them that they are dealing with someone who is serious about success and determined to build a business that will generate revenues far beyond the amount of the investment required.[13]

The nine building blocks are a great discipline to define and refine a business plan or revenue model. Notwithstanding, I offer a few additional practical thoughts for your consideration.

Where possible, try to identify the requisite operating, financial, and strategic critical mass and timing to position the company for a possible trade sale to a sector leader. Imagine the minimum 10 percent "threshold" that a potential acquirer's management or board of directors will be seeking in order to be moved to action.

Know that despite all the planning, young companies can die a thousand deaths every day, and are faced with multiple sliding doors of challenges and opportunities. As such, plans need to be flexible and adaptive.

Management at the helm whom have had prior VC-backed entrepreneurial experience through a successful exit, can make all the difference in navigating through the multiple challenges and opportunities.

Pick the right value-add VC, not just one that provides financing; this can have an exponentially positive impact on the company's survival rate and ability to optimize the value at exit.

Despite all the planning, one never knows where or when the viral event will materialize. Success just seems to repeat itself more often when you couple repeat entrepreneurs with value-adding VCs.

The Stark Reality of the Post-2008 Landscape

Whether a VC is looking to attract LPs, or a private company is striving to identify VC backing, it is a fact that there has been less money available for venture capital in the last decade. A lot of that has to do with the state of the economy since the 2008 implosion of the mortgage-backed securities bubble. This crisis was caused in large part by fraud and incompetence at all levels. Regulators and legislators have tried to put safeguards in place, but have really done little except create more paperwork and reporting requirements. As always, the principle of *caveat emptor* serves as the guiding light, and nowhere is this becoming more obvious than in the finance industry. Background checks have always been standard procedure as part of the VC's due diligence process, but now the trend has escalated to full background investigations by licensed, experienced security professionals. The potential portfolio company manager can expect a thorough investigation and validation of his work history, educational background, criminal background, community involvement, board service, and assets. Before you receive any funding in today's climate, the GP has to be able to show the LPs that you are a clean, upstanding individual with character and integrity. Investigators are going to look for legal entanglements, tax issues, corporate or personal bankruptcy, drug or alcohol problems, extramarital affairs, gambling issues, or any history of aberrant behavior. Your social media activity is going to be gone over thoroughly with any questionable posts or photographs noted. Remember, you are being selected for a long-term, very close working relationship and being entrusted with a substantial investment. If you cheat at golf or lie about your military exploits, you might be qualified to run for political office, but you might not be the most dependable business partner.

The assumptions in your business plan or business model will be thoroughly examined during the due diligence process.

This is where the business model has a clear advantage over the traditional business plan. Questions about your value proposition, the stage of your product or service development, market acceptance, and growth potential will have been thoroughly analyzed and fleshed out in the business model exercise, whereas the business plan will usually be a series of assumptions and ambitions supported by favorable data and subjective conclusions.

Intellectual property (IP) will become a particularly sensitive issue during this process. The entrepreneur has to be ready, willing, and able to document ownership, title, assignments, license agreements, and technical and geographic scope of protection. Are there any infringement issues or blocking patents? Can the IP withstand a litigious assault?

Finally, the early- or expansion-stage company's financials and organizational documentation will be scrutinized. For the companies, the financials are known guesstimates; however, there should be milestones and a reasonable allocation of capital aimed at reaching value creation. With the companies, test pricing and revenue assumptions are going to be looked at with the intention to improve gross margins.

The company organizational document package should include:

- The corporate charter and bylaws
- Founders and management agreements with any stock option plans

- Capitalization table (a list of who owns what)
- Any IP documentation
- Any real property documentation, including leases and estimates for capital improvements
- Three years' worth of current financial records and tax returns for all principals
- Investor agreements and equity-related communications with initial investors
- Material contracts, distribution and supplier agreements
- All required insurance policies
- Any contingent legal liability issues[14]

What's It Worth?

There have been volumes written on the subject of valuation of the enterprise, both from the viewpoint of the entrepreneur and from the VC's perspective. This book is not designed to get into the intricacies of the subject, but only to give the reader some basic framework from which to begin understanding this process. It is important that the entrepreneur understand such terms as *dilution* and *equity overhang*.

Dilution occurs when an additional class of shareholders is created. In other words, the pie is sliced into a greater number of slices, but is hopefully worth more. Somebody's slice is going to necessarily get smaller or be diluted. Overhang is an accounting of all of the promises and stakes that have been created for those who had enough faith in your idea to provide the initial ingredients to make the pie. That is why the VC wants you to provide your capitalization table and all of the investor agreements, promissory notes, and e-mails in which you promised Aunt Margaret 10 percent equity in your new company in exchange for the $50,000 she pulled out of her retirement account to help you build your first prototype.

The VC is trying to determine an accurate price for your enterprise, not just because he wants to get the largest percentage of ownership for the least amount of money. He does, but he is also looking further down the road. His experience tells him that you are going to probably need one or two more rounds of financing before you reach a point of growth where your revenue generation is going to support a profitable exit. This initial round of financing carries a higher risk and warrants a higher reward than the one for later-round investors who will be providing operational capital for a going concern. He doesn't want any surprises as the value of the enterprise begins to grow above and beyond the price being paid for the initial equity stake. And he certainly does not want his slice of the pie to get smaller.

Once the VC is convinced to proceed with capitalizing the venture, he will present the entrepreneur with a document called a Term Sheet. It is exactly what the title implies. Each of the clauses or terms of the document defines the terms under which the funds will be committed to the venture, arrangements for how the VC will hold its interest in the venture, the issues yet to be resolved in order to complete the transaction, and the terms defining the exclusivity of the VC's involvement and the protection of his interests going forward. It lays out the path forward for both parties and ensures that all parties to the transaction have a full understanding of their roles, responsibilities, and expectations. It lays the groundwork for future syndication and charts the course toward the ultimate goal: the successful exit.

The important terms fall into one of two categories; economic terms and control terms. Besides price or valuation, the important economic terms are *liquidation preference*, *pay-to-play*, *vesting*, *employee pool*, and *anti-dilution provisions*.

A Seat at the Table

The control parameters of the deal start with a clause aimed at allowing the VC to have at least one seat on the board of directors of the new venture. Having a VC with demonstrated sector experience on your board can be very helpful. The important thing is to maintain balance. Yes, the VC is providing the capital and has a vested interest in watching over how his investment is deployed; however, it is still your company. A common solution is to have a small board with an odd number of directors; half representing the founder, half representing the VC's interests, and the odd member being legitimately nonconflicted and with relevant industry experience.

Protective provisions in the Term Sheet are veto rights that the investors have over actions by the company that would have an adverse impact on the investor's position. Examples of such actions include creating more stock, selling the company, or borrowing more money. The drag-along agreement means that the founders and common stock holders agree to go along with a liquidity event that the VC initiates. The conversion clause gives preferred shareholders the right to convert their stock into common stock.

Other terms which are typically contained in the Term Sheet include but are not limited to dividends, right of first refusal, redemption rights, registration rights, and voting rights among others. Finally, the Term Sheet will also contain an updated version of the Capitalization Table showing the addition of all investors.

The Paperwork

The Term Sheet is the basis for all other legal documents that will be generated to finalize the investment. It's great to have a good attorney, and we advise you to engage the most competent professional guidance possible, but it ultimately comes down to you taking the time and making the effort to educate yourself. Ask questions. If there is something you do not understand, ask for an explanation in language that you can understand. If you still have concerns, don't hesitate to get a second opinion. If not, walk away!

Final Word

To summarize, the following takeaways offer some pretty fail-safe and time-tested tenets to aid in the diligence and selection process, and that apply to most VC-related GPs, LPs, and entrepreneurs.

- Always look to ensure that the economic interests of the LP, GP, and the entrepreneurs are aligned.
- Make sure that all parties have meaningful "skin in the game."
- Seek assurance that the proposed fund or venture is led by managers or entrepreneurs with track records that are highly correlated and relevant to the proposed investment strategy or business plan.
- Where possible, look for repeated successes in track records, not just one hit wonders. Look for management teams consisting of balanced and complementary contributors, not just the single star performer.
- Identify the institutional investor who is leading the financial transaction, and she will serve as the LP representative to monitor the investment.

Chapter Nine

Investment Process—Portfolio Construction, Monitoring, and Monetizing

I love the ability to work with very good managers, and to provide the right incentives for them, and truly become a partner with that management, and make that management take a long view.

—Henry Kravis, co-founder of private equity firm, Kohlberg Kravis Roberts & Co. (KKR)

Some Important Words on Portfolio Construction

Asset allocation and portfolio construction guidelines are absolutely essential to ensure that an investor's dollar allocation to the VC asset class and its make-up are "right-sized/right-fit" to the intended investment holding period.

The first step in the process is to assess the investor's financial resources and capability, their risk profile, and appetite to absorb risk.

Next is a decision with regard to the percentage portfolio allocation to the VC asset class. Although varying widely, investor-by-investor, your author has suggested an efficient frontier target of 12 to 15 percent.

In this and the two preceding chapters the investor's prescribed selection criteria are discussed in detail. As discussed, VC is in most cases not a liquid asset class, so it becomes important to utilize a dollar-averaged approach towards making the allocation, initially targeting a five-year period, and thereafter continuing to make annual investment allocations to maintain the efficient frontier threshold.

It is also critical to add diversity to the portfolio, where 10 to 20 percent limits are maintained regarding individual allocations, for example, listed versus private holdings, stages of investment maturity, industry or sector focus, geography and investment strategies—all of which we have discussed in prior chapters. Diversification is also important in that the VC portfolio asset allocation produces the desired benefit of being statistically non-correlated to the investor's more traditional investment portfolio asset classes.

Finally, the investor should always seek to identify the liquidity event, or exit, and establish a goal for their desired investment returns. As mentioned earlier, the VC asset class is best held as a long-term investment, with expectations that it deliver more than 600 basis points of incremental return annually compared to the traditional asset classes.

Monitoring

TheFunded.com (www.thefunded.com) is an online community that allows entrepreneurs to research, rate, and review venture funds from around the world. The site lists contact information and anonymous feedback ratings for over 4,000 funds. Of its 18,000 members, approximately 95 percent are CEOs of start-ups. In 2007, the website rated Fred Wilson, a managing partner and co-founder of Union Square Ventures (www.usv.com), as their favorite venture capitalist (VC). Wilson is a New York City–based venture capitalist and blogger. His firm has famously invested in Web 2.0 companies such as Twitter, Tumblr, Foursquare, Zynga, Kickstarter, and 10gen. In his blog,

"A VC—Musings of a VC in NYC" (www.avc.com), Wilson once commented on the role of the VC after the investment takes place.

> Investing in management means building communication systems, business processes, feedback, and routines that let you scale the business and team as efficiently as possible.

A variation on the Golden Rule says, "He who has the gold makes the rules." Nowhere is this more true than in the world of venture capital investing. The reasons are that the VC, in the role of general partner, has a fiduciary responsibility to the limited partners to do everything he can to ensure that the capital invested is used for the purposes intended and that everyone involved is focused on the principal goal of obtaining a satisfactory return on investment. This begins and ends with the VC's participation in the guidance, growth, and management of the new start-up by taking a seat on the firm's board of directors. The Golden Rule is of course most often achieved where VCs apply it with their skill to align company management's support in achieving the goal.

It is during the monitoring and monetization process where the VC's true value-add to the company occurs and where the more skilled VCs are differentiated from the empty suits.

Duties of a Board of Directors

The Term Sheet almost always spells out the voting rights of each class of stockholder in the company and the composition of the board of directors of the company. Typically, the lead investor, as a holder of Series A preferred stock, always gets at least one seat on the board if for no other reason than to keep an eye on how the money is spent. A board member is not just an honorary position that a founder gives to his friends and family. Board members have a moral, ethical, and often legal requirement to exercise a reasonable amount of care in the performance of their duties. These duties include, at their most basic level, the identification and creation of the value proposition of the company, sustaining that value, and guiding the management and resources of the company toward realization of that value via a liquidity event.

The most common practice is to have an odd number of directors divided fairly evenly between the vision of the founder and the demands of the investor with a neutral, unaligned director to serve as the unbiased and objective voice of reason. Good board members are hard to find, and the founder should do all within his power to ensure that the board is a qualified and effective resource that can be depended upon to render sound judgment and solid strategic planning advice. Even if the VC insists on having multiple board seats, the founder can be equally as insistent that they have sector or industry expertise at a minimum.

The National Association of Corporate Directors (NACD) is a very good resource for a founder. NACD's mission is to advance exemplary board leadership—for directors, by directors—by delivering the knowledge and insight that board members need to confidently navigate complex business challenges and enhance shareowner value. Their website (www.nacdonline.org) contains a great many resources to enhance boardroom intelligence, improve board performance, and provide ongoing and current dialogue on regulatory and legislative issues. The NACD Knowledge Base is a vast repository of corporate governance resources, which includes archives of articles, templates, tools, whitepapers, sample charters, and other advisory documents. These cover such topics as audit and finance, strategy and risk, board composition, policies and procedures, director liability, government, compensation, CEO performance management and succession, and roles of the board and management.

A good example of the information available from the NACD is a 2013 report entitled "Bridging Effectiveness Gaps: A Candid Look at Board Practices," in which the authors address the board's responsibility regarding issues of strategy and risk.

Overseeing a company's strategy is perhaps a board's most important duty. For many years, respondent directors of the annual NACD Public Company Governance Survey identified "strategic planning and oversight" as their top priority. Recently, the survey participants also ranked "risk and crisis oversight" in the top three. The importance of these issues is unmistakable. A director's primary duty is to ensure the long-term sustainability and profitability of the company while increasing shareholder returns.

The existence of a good corporate strategy is crucial to seeing it through. Subsequently, a significant portion of a board's time should be spent reflecting on corporate strategy and the potential risks involved. This, however, is not always the case. Board meeting agendas are stocked with issues requiring board attention, especially compliance matters. Many directors find that not enough time is given to the critical business issues needing director input, such as corporate strategy and performance. Many directors indicate that there is a limited amount of time to understand the risks facing a company and that it is difficult for some directors to add significant value to discussions. Given the fact that boards average 5.5 meetings per year and dedicate only 6.5 hours per meeting, it is not surprising that directors find it difficult to address all the most important issues facing the board.[1]

When considering the makeup of the board, it is important to keep in mind the perception gap between what the C-suite deals with on a daily basis versus what the board only glimpses periodically. This is especially important with respect to strategy and risk. For some reason, the CEO paradigm has become the confident Master and Commander, who can handle all challenges and face all risk with aplomb and a smile. Admission of risk is seen as a weakness. This is unfortunate because it can hamper the board's ability to provide wisdom and understanding in dealing with issues like strategic risk. The board can be a CEO's valuable asset when developing strategies and exploring possible contingencies.

The C-suite is the highest level of executives in an organization. The appellation refers to the three-letter initials starting with "C" and ending with "O," as in "Chief . . . Officer," which traditionally are the chief executive officer (CEO), chief operations officer (COO), and the chief financial officer (CFO). Many technology-based companies have a chief technology officer (CTO), and many service-oriented companies have a chief marketing officer (CMO). These are the individuals responsible for the particular facet of the company under their purview, with the CEO being considered the highest ranking corporate officer and answerable only to the board of directors.

More often than not, it is during the informal, one-on-one conversations between individual board members and the C-suite executives where the individual board members may be able to add value. During the informal start-up or early stage of the company, board members may have the opportunity to turn a challenge that occurs during daily operations as a teaching moment or the chance to share expertise and suggest alternatives that can add tremendous value to the operation overall.

Another organization that can be an excellent resource for the founder is The Working Group on Director Accountability and Board Effectiveness, a member association of venture capitalists, CEOs, and industry thought leaders put together by Pascal Levensohn. He is the founder and managing partner of Levensohn Venture Partners LLC (LVP), an early- and development-stage venture capital firm based in San Francisco. In their 2007 white paper entitled "A Simple Guide to the Basic Responsibilities of VC-Backed Company Directors," the group points out:

> First-time entrepreneurs who become founding CEOs frequently become corporate directors even before they obtain their first institutional

round of venture capital financing. While taking venture capital ("VC") is always a choice, there is no opting out of the legal responsibilities of corporate directors.[2]

The report points out that the boards of venture capital–backed companies (VCBC) are unique in that they have to face challenges across four distinct stages. These are:

1. Seed funding and product/technology/service development
2. Early commercialization
3. Late stage expansion
4. Liquidity through either an acquisition or an initial public offering (IPO)

For the purposes of our discussion of monitoring of the portfolio company by the VC, we will focus only upon the last stage. During preparation for monetization, or a liquidity event, the board's focus changes to management of growth, profitability, and gross margins. There is a greater interface with and focus upon investor relations, legal, compliance, and professional management. Even if not pursuing an IPO exit, the board begins to adopt a more public-like demeanor with the establishment of internal controls, standards, and practices, and the implementation of Section 404 planning.[3] Section 404 of the Sarbanes-Oxley Act (SOX) requires public companies' annual reports to include the company's own assessment of internal control over financial reporting and an auditor's attestation. As we stated before, the financial burden of overbearing and ineffective legislation is something that needs to become a priority of those we elect and those who are appointed ostensibly to serve the public good.

Communication

The key to successful management is good communication. This begins right from the initial phases of building your business model. As the founder or visionary, you have to be able to mobilize the necessary assets and resources you need to succeed. This begins with being able to convey your idea in such a manner that it inspires others to join you in your quest and to marshal the energy, time, focus, and knowledge that you need to define your business, identify your market, and develop your value proposition.

The way to get the board and the management team aligned is to open the lines of communication to ensure that you have a constant, open dialogue between the board and senior management. This starts with the tone at the top. The CEO should encourage the board to get to know the management team and to freely ask questions inside and outside of the boardroom. This helps to further refine and implement the business model by providing a bilateral communication channel for proposing ideas and hypotheses with immediate feedback and analysis.

As the company matures, the business model paradigm allows for the board and the C-suite to actively monitor the company's reaction to the ever-changing business environment, engage stakeholders, launch innovation, redesign projects, and track the company's overall health indicators in a timely manner. These indicators include the financial data, sales metrics, and customer feedback. They should also include internal channels for submitting ideas and feedback from employees. A truly successful leader attracts gifted people, and there should be no restrictions on where great ideas or suggestions can come from.

Processes, Systems, Roles, and Responsibilities

Another mark of a successful operation is a clear understanding of how a company creates its product or provides it service. Here is where the business model shows its full value. Every key resource is identified, every key activity is defined, and every key relationship is assigned to a particular person in the organization. Going through the exercise of fully fleshing out and assigning responsibilities for the various segments of the business model canvas adds value, by building an organization of people who are not only empowered to perform a requisite task, but who also know how the proper execution of that task interacts with the rest of the organization and the outcomes that are expected of them.

During the early stages of growth, this becomes a critical tool for maintaining focus and instilling accountability. It builds organizational knowledge, which establishes an identifiable culture as the business grows and departments become formalized and insular. By establishing an outcome-based awareness early on, the board of directors no longer represents an isolated entity of outsiders and meddlers, but becomes a trusted source of guidance and vision for the entire organization.

As the company reaches the point of considering a liquidity event, there develops awareness within the internal community of every person's role and responsibility. No matter the title on the door or the position in the organization chart, everyone from the CEO to the shipping clerk understands their importance to the success of the overall enterprise.

Course Adjustments

One of the biggest fears of many entrepreneurs is having their vision proven wrong. This is unfortunate because one of America's greatest innovators, Thomas Edison, proved conclusively that failure is necessary for success. Vision, intuition, and judgment are crucial human elements of entrepreneurial success, but they can also be key factors in the demise of a once-great idea. Ideas like Microsoft's purchase of WebTV in 1997 had to be approved by a board of directors who had apparently lost their focus. The introduction of

New Coke revealed a CEO who, in the minds of many, had stopped listening to the customer. Both revealed organizational leadership who had lost sight of the organization's goals. If such problems can happen to two established business powerhouses, they can easily happen to a young venture still discovering and defining its place in the market.

Establishment of good communication channels and well-defined roles and responsibilities can serve to keep the board and the C-suite accountable and focused on the corporate goal. By maintaining a beginner's mindset, entrepreneurs can take advantage of synergies that arise, abate conflicts that emerge, and generally avoid becoming victims of their own success. By continually testing the hypotheses in your business model, analyzing the feedback from your customers, and reiterating your product or service offering, you can change course with confidence, if needed. Vision, intuition, and judgment must always be tempered to align with the organization's prime directive—reaching the liquidity event.

Cut Losses Early

This is the most important differentiator of the "best from the rest" VCs. Here, the more experienced and proficient VC has the ability to size up the winners from the rest of the pack fairly early on after investment. He can focus his value-add attention on the winners and seek monetization alternatives for the rest, whether by secondary sale, strategic sale, or shutdown of the venture.

This is easier said than done. It is very difficult to admit to your GP partners and LPs that you got it wrong or that you were fooled into funding a venture that really had no chance of performing as projected. The path of least resistance for most VCs in this situation is known as management by neglect. It means simply ignoring the operation and allowing it to sink of its own accord. If it should happen to turn things around and get back on course, the VC looks like the long-shot hero.

In the July/August edition of *Inc.* magazine, Eric Paley weighs in on what a founder needs to do in order to avoid being fired from the company he created. Paley, a veteran entrepreneur and managing partner of the $110 million seed stage venture fund Founder Collective (http://foundercollective.com), says that replacement of the founder happens more frequently than most people realize. It is never an easy decision for a board to make. The founder is usually the visionary who was able to get the VC excited enough to invest in the first place; however, the board has an obligation to do what is in the best interest of the investors.

What are some typical offenses that can lead to termination? The most frequent one, according to Paley, is the other side of the "visionary" coin: the inability to proper deal with the cold, hard facts of reality. Whether it is fear of failure or paralysis by analysis, a CEO soon loses credibility if he fails to accurately evaluate whether the company is performing as required and meeting its objectives. This type of failure can quickly undermine the morale and effectiveness of every employee and bring an organization to its knees. Rose-colored glasses are never an acceptable fashion accessory for a successful leader.

Another stumbling block for newly minted CEOs is the requirement to handle tasks that are outside one's normal field of competence. A great organization requires many different functions to operate in synchronous harmony and efficiency. Administration, legal, product development, sales, marketing, finance, accounting, public relations, production, procurement, and logistics are all areas that require the CEO's attention, awareness, and some acumen. Many founders come from product development backgrounds and are not adept at team building, managing expectations, or adroitly maneuvering through the political landscape of a modern organization. A great leader knows her limitations and surrounds herself with people who can fill in those gaps and get the job done. Failing to recognize one's lack of competence or failure to build a senior team to lead the different functions of the organization are both offenses that can lead to axing the CEO.[4]

A great VC will identify and act on this early on and address this problem by identifying a COO, a Mr. Fix-It to work alongside the CEO or president. To put this into perspective, it is not an admission of being bad at picking the right people to manage companies, but rather the challenge for VCs and CEOs alike is to manage early-stage companies in very rapidly changing marketplaces. There are only a handful of founding CEOs who actually remain CEOs of companies that go on to achieve $1 billion or more in annual sales.

These red flags are spotted early by the experienced VC and trigger appropriate intervention measures. This usually begins with a private conversation and inquiries into awareness of issues on the part of the CEO. Hopefully, this is all that is needed; however, the VC must see a quick and effective response with quantifiable results.

Another important red flag is not reaching the identified company milestones required to achieve the critical mass necessary to position for a liquidity event. Here, the VC quickly discerns and acts on what are legitimate market-driven catalysts requiring the reset button to be hit as compared to senior management excuses for lack of performance.

Lastly, the company burn rate can be an early indicator. This is the rate at which an organization is using up its shareholder capital. It is also known as negative cash flow. If the shareholder capital is exhausted, the company will either have to start making a profit, find additional funding, or close down. If the company is making adequate progress and the VC has anticipated the need for additional funding, the burn rate is considered manageable. If it is not, the VC has no choice but to cut its losses. The operation will be shut down, and all assets will be liquidated in order to recover as much of the initial investment as possible. The power of the purse is supreme.

Methods of Monetization

Liquidation events or exits are situations that can test the mettle of even the most experienced venture capitalist. Many competing interests have to be brought together in just the right manner, under the right set of circumstances, to allow investors to exit the venture successfully. First of all, the company must be ready to be exited, meaning that it has matured to the point where it is profitable and has created enough value to be attractive to either the public market or a potential suitor. Supply and demand conditions must be aligned so that somebody wants to buy the company or the markets are willing to accept it.

The needs of the investors also have to be taken into consideration with respect to the timing of an exit. The state of the economy often plays a role when either the GP or the LPs find themselves in the position of needing to create liquidity and begin to urge a company to exit earlier than planned, often at a lower price than originally desired.

In the end, the most common trigger for a liquidity event is that the company has grown to a point where the value added by the VC's efforts is less than the projected cost of the effort. Assuming that the investors and the board are in agreement with this assessment, the issue then becomes which course of action to take to exit the investment.[5]

Mergers and Acquisitions

An acquisition is the most popular form of exit in the venture capital/private equity industries in the United States. In fact, according to a 2011 report by Ernst & Young, M&A makes up as much as 90 percent of U.S. VC-backed exits.

> With many cash-rich U.S. businesses focused on organic growth, companies are expected to look to acquisitions and increase their focus on divestitures as a way to maximize shareholder value, raise capital, or generate growth. M&A deal activity is expected to moderately strengthen for 2012 and beyond.
>
> Larger deals but fewer transactions characterize the M&A market. In 2011, there were 477 VC-backed M&A deals worth an aggregate $47.8 billion, representing a 23 percent rise in capital and a 15% decrease in deal numbers compared with the same period in 2010. (In 2010, the venture-backed M&A market in the United States recorded its first rise in both deal numbers and value since the peaks

of 2007, with 560 deals generating $39.0 billion, almost 69 percent higher than in 2009.)

M&A valuations are quite strong and offer broad investor participation, with capital efficiency on par with the pre-Internet bubble period. Driving the acquisitions momentum is the recognition by large corporations that they cannot generate all of the innovation they need internally, and that they need to partner with VC firms and their portfolio companies to access external innovation relevant to their businesses. In addition, with a generally soft IPO market, valuations for many companies are low, making acquisitions attractive to large cash-rich corporations. The main exit route for VC-backed companies in Western countries is acquisitions (M&A), representing 80 percent to 90 percent of all exits.[6]

Acquisitions are preferred due to the speed and efficiency with which the transaction can be completed. There are also fewer regulatory hurdles with which to contend. Larger companies find it much more efficient to purchase a start-up technology provider than to invest in the commitment of resources that accompanies internal R&D.

Key drivers for acquisitions are a fast improvement in revenues and profitability, operational synergies that improve the value proposition, diversification of product or service offerings, geographic penetration into new markets, and the aggrandizement of any new developments that might have the potential to become a future threat to market share.

That does not mean that acquisitions are always successful. Many transactions falter due to price issues, terms and conditions placed upon the sale, the amount of risk involved, and third-party challenges on regulatory and legal issues such as monopolistic positioning or revelation of classified technologies.[7]

Initial Public Offering (IPO)

Many entrepreneurs see an initial public offering (IPO) or stock market launch as the pinnacle of success. Popular media have conditioned most business types to see the IPO as a great achievement; however, recent changes in the regulatory environment and economic realities have taken some of the luster off the IPO. Although an IPO offers many advantages, there are also significant disadvantages. Chief among these are the increased regulatory burdens that come with being a publically traded company, the costs associated with the process, and the requirement to disclose certain information that could prove helpful to competitors, or create difficulties with vendors.

From 1980 to 2000, an annual average of 310 operating companies went public in the United States. From 2001 to

2011, only 30 percent of that number of companies went public in spite of the doubling of real gross domestic product (GDP) during this 32-year period. The decline has been even more severe for small company initial public offerings (IPOs), for which the average volume has dropped from 166 IPOs per year during 1980–2000 to only 29 per year during 2001–2011, a drop of 83 percent. The reasons for such a dramatic drop are commonly thought to be the costs associated with the onerous burden of regulations like Sarbanes-Oxley; but that may not be the real reason. A 2012 study by University of Florida finance professor, Jay Ritter, puts forth the economies of scope hypothesis. He posits that there is an ongoing change in the economy that has reduced the profitability of small companies, whether public or private. The findings of the research he conducted with Xiaohui Gao of the University of Hong Kong and Zhongyan Zhu of the Chinese University of Hong Kong, contend that many small firms can create greater operating profits through an acquisition rather than operating as an independent firm and relying on organic growth. A larger organization can realize economies of scope and bring new technology to market faster.[8]

Another deterrent to small company IPOs is the discount offered by investment bankers who help establish the initial share price by arranging opening day sales of blocks of shares to institutional investors. This is typically about 15 percent below the opening day price. To get around this several smaller companies have used a technique called a Dutch auction to establish the opening day price.

A Dutch auction is a process whereby individual investors log onto their brokerage accounts and bid for a certain number of shares or bid a certain amount toward the purchase of shares. After the auction was completed, the company would establish the fair market value price of the stock, and the bidders would receive the appropriate number of shares. The most notable recent example of this method is the Google IPO, which angered the Wall Street establishment. In the case of Google, the winners turned out to be the individual investors, who are normally shut out of the better IPO deals by the Wall Street insiders.[9]

Secondary Sales

Unlike IPOs and trade sales, secondary markets operate at the individual investor level rather than at the start-up level. Because investors have different liquidity needs, an individual-investor option offers exit to those who need it—for example, to the serial entrepreneur who wishes to start another venture or to the VC whose fund is about to expire and who must return capital to his investors.

Secondary buyers who take their place will have a fresh exit clock, a discounted purchase price, and the opportunity to invest in an asset class that was previously unavailable to them, which includes some of the world's most promising companies. Not only do secondary markets make for more efficient outcomes at the individual-investor level, but they also lead to more efficient outcomes for start-ups, which will no longer be forced into premature, traditional exits to satisfy an individual investor's liquidity needs.[10]

Recapitalization

Another alternative may be the reorganization of a portfolio company's debt and equity mixture, called a recapitalization. The VC exchanges its equity for cash, the management team gains equity incentives, and the company is positioned for future growth. Slow maturation may cause some LPs to want to exit the investment early in order to go after more exciting or promising ventures. This becomes problematic when the founder is particularly charismatic or the GP is committed to the point of wanting to double down on the initial investment. This often happens in the case of biotechnology companies where, for instance, the clinical trials and testing that consumed most of the initial capital reveals that the drug under development would be exponentially more efficacious and profitable if marketed for a completely different condition.

Recapitalizations can often take the form of a roll-up, whereby the early-stage VC sells his interest in a portfolio company to an expansion-stage VC or SME-stage PE fund, whose investment strategy and expertise is to use the company as a platform from which to grow through accretion.

Winding Up

The process of winding up consists of selling all the assets of a business, paying off creditors, distributing any remaining assets to the principals or parent company, and then dissolving the business. Winding up can refer to such a process either for a specific business line of a corporation or to the dissolution of a corporation itself. This is not always a winning strategy for the VC because there may additional costs involved, including severance pay, taxes, lease payoffs on facilities and equipment, and even cleanup and cartage fees. All good things must come to an end, but that doesn't mean that all things necessarily come to a good end.

Conclusion: Is VC Still Alive?

Ever since World War II, the United States has been the world's most important growth machine. This growth machine's three most powerful pistons—capital markets, innovation, and the knowledge economy—have in fact been sputtering for a decade.

The United States once boasted the world's most business friendly capital markets. VCs have, in fact, slashed their spending, where the number of IPOs is down from an average of 547 a year in the 1990s to 192 since then. This has dramatically cut the supply of new, high-growth companies. Given that companies less than five years old have provided the vast majority of the 40 million net jobs the American economy added between 1980 and the 2007–2008 financial crisis, this is dismal news for the unemployed.

America used to have one of the most business-friendly immigration policies: 18 percent of the Fortune 500 companies as of 2010 were founded by immigrants (including AT&T, DuPont, eBay, Google, Kraft, Heinz, and P&G). If you include the children of immigrants the figure is 40 percent. In fact, immigrants have founded 25 percent of the successful high-tech and engineering companies between 1995 and 2005. They obtain patents at twice the rate of American-born people with the same educational credentials. But American immigration policies have tightened dramatically over the past decade.

Finally, America has long boasted the world's most business-friendly universities. One-fifth of American start-ups are linked to universities, which have spawned businesses by the thousands. But the university-business boom seems to be fading. For example, federal spending on health-related research increased from $20 billion in 1993 to $30 billion in 2008, but the number of new drugs approved by the FDA fell from a peak of 50 in 1996 to just 15 in 2008. University technology offices, which legally have first dibs at commercializing the faculty's ideas, have evolved into clumsy bureaucracies. The average age of researchers given grants by the NIH is 50 and rising.

These problems all bear more heavily on entrepreneurs than on established companies. As such, American capitalism is becoming more like Europe's, established firms with scale to deal with a growing thicket of regulations are doing well, but new and SME-size companies are withering on the vine or selling themselves to incumbents.

What can be done to reverse this worrying trend? Messrs. Litan and Schramm provide detailed answers in their book, *Better Capitalism*. They note that the recent JOBS Act is a step in the right direction. The act exempts new companies, for their first five years, from the onerous time and costs associated with Sarbanes-Oxley (SOX) regulations passed in 2002, in response to a spate of corporate scandals (e.g., Enron, World Telecom, Tyson). The JOBS Act quadruples the number of shareholders that private companies can have (from 499 to 2,000) before they have to go public.

Also suggested, the government should give Green Cards to all foreigners who come to America to study science, technology, engineering, or math.

Furthermore, exchange-traded funds (ETFs), which have gone from nothing a decade ago to a trillion-dollar industry today, leave promising new companies vulnerable to the fickleness of high-frequency traders, so why not let small companies opt out from such baskets of shares? As SOX is reducing the supply of new companies in the name of protecting investors, why not let the smaller firms opt out so long as shareholders are duly warned? The authors also argue that university technology offices should lose their monopolies, giving professors more freedom to exploit their innovations.

These are all very sensible and practical arguments to ensure that America's entrepreneurs and VCs do not become an endangered species.

I believe that small business is the engine of our free enterprise economy, and venture capital is definitely the carburetor. Washington D.C. may put a lot of people to work in the bloated bureaucracies of our ever-expanding government or make-work infrastructure projects, but that is not creating wealth. It is increasing the load on the economy because every federal paycheck has to come from We the People. We are paying their salaries. We are paying their bonuses. We are even paying for their lavish trips to Las Vegas and elsewhere. Personally, I don't think we are getting our money's worth. I personally believe that venture capital investing creates businesses and jobs which put money into your pocket and brings your dreams into reality. I hope after reading this book, you agree.

Appendix: Resources

VC Glossary of Terms

We have provided a link to an online glossary of VC terms, www.altassets.net/private-equity-and-venture-capital-glossary-of-terms, which will help you understand important private equity and venture capital terms. Use the definitions to help yourself understand how the industry operates. Here are just a few.

acquisition The process of taking over a controlling interest in another company. Acquisition also describes any deal where the bidder ends up with 50 percent or more of the company taken over.

acquisition finance Companies often need to use external finance to fund an acquisition. This can be in the form of bank debt and/or equity, such as a share issue.

advisory board An advisory board is common among smaller companies. It is less formal than the board of directors. It usually consists of people, chosen by the company founders, whose experience, knowledge, and influence can benefit the growth and direction of the business. The board will meet periodically but does not have any legal responsibilities in regard to the company.

alternative assets This term describes nontraditional asset classes. They include private equity, venture capital, hedge funds, and real estate. Alternative assets are generally more risky than traditional assets, but they should, in theory, generate higher returns for investors.

angel investor See **business angels.**

asset Anything owned by an individual, a business or financial institution that has a present or future value; that is, can be turned into cash. In accounting terms, an asset is something of future economic benefit obtained as a result of previous transactions. Tangible assets can be land and buildings, fixtures, and fittings; examples of intangible assets are goodwill, patents, and copyrights.

asset allocation The percentage breakdown of an investment portfolio. This shows how the investment is divided among different asset classes. These classes include shares, bonds, property, cash, and overseas investments. Institutions structure their allocations to balance risk and ensure they have a diversified portfolio. The asset classes produce a range of returns—for example, bonds provide a low but steady return, equities a higher but riskier return. Cash has a guaranteed return. Effective asset allocation maximizes returns while covering liabilities.

balanced fund A fund that spreads its investments between various types of assets such as stocks and bonds. Investors can avoid excessive risk by balancing their investments in this manner, but should expect only moderate returns.

benchmark This is a standard measure used to assess the performance of a company. Investors need to know whether or not a company is hitting certain benchmarks, as this will determine the structure of the investment package. For example, a company that is slow to reach certain benchmarks may compensate investors by increasing their stock allocations.

bond A type of IOU issued by companies or institutions. They generally have a fixed interest rate and maturity value, so they're very low risk—much less risky than buying equity—but their returns are accordingly low.

bridge loan A kind of short-term financing that allows a company to continue running until it can arrange longer-term financing. Companies sometimes seek this because they run out of cash before they receive long-term funding; sometimes they do so to strengthen their balance sheet in the run-up to flotation.

burn rate The rate at which a start-up uses its venture capital funding before it begins earning any revenue.

business angels Individuals who provide seed or start-up finance to entrepreneurs in return for equity. Angels usually contribute a lot more than pure cash—they often have industry knowledge and contacts that they can pass on to entrepreneurs. Angels sometimes have non-executive directorships in the companies they invest in.

buy-out This is the purchase of a company or a controlling interest of a corporation's shares. This often happens when a company's existing managers wish to take control of the company. See **management buy-out.**

capital commitment Every investor in a private equity fund commits to investing a specified sum of money in the fund partnership over a specified period of time. The fund records this as the limited partnership's capital commitment. The sum of capital commitments is equal to the size of the fund. Limited partners and the general partner must make a capital commitment to participate in the fund.

capital distribution These are the returns that an investor in a private equity fund receives. It is the income and capital realized from investments less expenses and liabilities. Once a limited partner has had its cost of investment returned, further distributions are actual profit. The partnership agreement determines the timing of distributions to the limited partner. It will also determine how profits are divided among the limited partners and general partner.

capital gain When an asset is sold for more than the initial purchase cost, the profit is known as the capital gain. This is the opposite of capital loss, which occurs when an asset is sold for less than the initial purchase price. Capital gain refers strictly to the gain achieved once an asset has been sold—an unrealized capital gain refers to an asset that could potentially produce a gain if it was sold. An investor will not necessarily receive the full value of the capital gain—capital gains are often taxed; the exact amount will depend on the specific tax regime.

capital under management This is the amount of capital that the fund has at its disposal and is managing for investment purposes.

carried interest The share of profits that the fund manager is due once it has returned the cost of investment to investors. Carried interest is normally expressed as a percentage of the total profits of the fund. The industry norm is 20 percent. The fund manager will normally receive 20 percent of the profits generated by the fund and distribute the remaining 80 percent of the profits to investors.

clawback A clawback provision ensures that a general partner does not receive more than its agreed percentage of carried interest over the life of the fund. So, for example, if a general partner receives 21 percent of the partnership's profits instead of the agreed 20 percent, limited partners can clawback the extra 1 percent.

closing This term can be confusing. If a fund-raising firm announces it has reached first or second closing, it doesn't mean that it is not seeking further investment. When fund raising, a firm will announce a first closing to release or drawdown the money raised so far so that it can start investing. A fund may have many closings, but the usual number is around three. Only when a firm announces a final closing is it no longer open to new investors.

co-investment Although used loosely to describe any two parties that invest alongside each other in the same company, this term has a special meaning when referring to limited partners in a fund. If a limited partner in a fund has co-investment rights, it can invest directly in a company that is also backed by the private equity fund. The institution therefore ends up with two separate stakes in the company—one indirectly through the fund; one directly in the company. Some private equity firms offer co-investment rights to encourage institutions to invest in their funds.

The advantage for an institution is that it should see a higher return than if it invested all its private equity allocation in funds—it doesn't have to pay a management fee and won't see at least 20 percent of its return swallowed by a fund's carried interest. But to co-invest successfully, institutions need to have sufficient knowledge of the market to assess whether a co-investment opportunity is a good one.

corporate venturing This is the process by which large companies invest in smaller companies. They usually do this for strategic reasons. For example, a large corporation such as Nokia may invest in smaller technology companies that are developing new products that can be assimilated into the Nokia product range. A large pharmaceutical company might invest in R&D centers on the basis that they get first refusal of research findings.

debt financing This is raising money for working capital or capital expenditure through some form of loan. This could be by arranging a bank loan or by selling bonds, bills, or notes (forms of debt) to individuals or institutional investors. In return for lending the money, the individuals or institutions become creditors and receive a promise to repay principal plus interest on the debt.

distressed debt (otherwise known as vulture capital) This is a form of finance used to purchase the corporate bonds of companies that have either filed for bankruptcy or appear likely to do so. Private equity firms and other corporate financiers who buy distressed debt don't asset-strip and liquidate the companies they purchase. Instead, they can make good returns by restoring them to health and then prosperity. These buyers first become a major creditor of the target company. This gives them leverage to play a prominent role in the reorganization or liquidation stage.

distribution in specie/distribution in kind This can happen if an investment has resulted in an IPO. A limited partner may receive its return in the form of stock or securities instead of cash. This can be controversial. The stock may not be liquid, and limited partners can be left with shares that are worth a fraction of the amount they would have received in cash. There can also be restrictions in the United States about how soon a limited partner can sell the stock (Rule 144). This means that sometimes the share value has decreased by the time the limited partner is legally allowed to sell.

drawdown When a venture capital firm has decided where it would like to invest, it will approach its own investors in order to draw down the money. The money will already have been pledged to the fund, but this is the actual act of transferring the money so that it reaches the investment target.

due diligence Investing successfully in private equity at a fund or company level involves thorough investigation. As a long-term investment, it is essential to review and analyze all aspects of the deal before signing. Capabilities of the management team, performance record, deal flow, investment strategy, and legal aspects are examples of areas that are fully examined during the due diligence process.

early-stage finance This is the realm of the venture capital—as opposed to the private equity—firm. A venture capitalist will normally invest in a company when it is in an early stage of development. This means that the company has only recently been established, or is still in the process of being established—it needs capital to develop and to become profitable. Early-stage finance is risky because it's often unclear how the market will respond to a new company's concept. However, if the venture is successful, the venture capitalist's return is correspondingly high.

equity financing Companies seeking to raise finance may use equity financing instead of or in addition to debt financing. To raise equity finance, a company creates new ordinary shares and sells them for cash. The new share owners become part owners of the company and share in the risks and rewards of the company's business.

exit Private equity professionals have their eyes on the exit from the moment they first see a business plan. An exit is the means by which a fund is able to realize its investment in a company—by an initial public offering, a trade sale, selling to another private equity firm, or a company buy-back. If a fund manager can't see an obvious exit route in a potential investment, then it won't touch it. A fund has the power to force an investee company to sell up so that it can exit the investment and make its profit, but venture capitalists claim this is rare—the exit is usually agreed upon with the company's management team.

fund of funds A fund set up to distribute investments among a selection of private equity fund managers, who in turn invest the capital directly. Fund of funds are specialist private equity investors and have existing relationships with firms. They may be able to provide investors with a route to investing in particular funds that would otherwise be closed to them. Investing in fund of funds can also help spread the risk of investing in private equity because they invest the capital in a variety of funds.

fund raising The process by which a private equity firm solicits financial commitments from limited partners for a fund. Firms typically set a target when they begin raising the fund and ultimately announce that the fund has closed at such-and-such amount. This may mean that no additional capital will be accepted. But sometimes the firms will have multiple interim closings each time they have hit particular targets (first closings, second closings, etc.) and final closings. The term cap is the maximum amount of capital a firm will accept in its fund.

general partner This can refer to the top-ranking partners at a private equity firm as well as the firm managing the private equity fund.

general partner contribution/commitment This is the amount of capital that the fund manager contributes to its own fund. This is an important way for limited partners to ensure that their interests are aligned with those of the general partner. The U.S. Department of the Treasury recently removed the legal requirement of the general partner to contribute at least 1 percent of fund capital, but this is still the usual contribution.

incubator An entity designed to nurture business ideas or new technologies to the point that they become attractive to venture capitalists. An incubator typically provides physical space and some or all of the services—legal, managerial, technical—needed for a business idea to be developed. Private equity firms often back incubators as a way of generating early-stage investment opportunities.

initial public offering (IPO) An IPO is the official term for going public. It occurs when a privately held company—owned, for example, by its founders plus perhaps its private equity investors—lists a proportion of its shares on a stock exchange. IPOs are an exit route for private equity firms. Companies that do an IPO are often relatively small and new and are seeking equity capital to expand their businesses.

internal rate of return (IRR) This is the most appropriate performance benchmark for private equity investments. In simple terms, it is a time-weighted return expressed as a percentage. IRR uses the present sum of cash drawdowns (money invested), the present value of distributions (money returned from investments), and the current value of unrealized investments and applies a discount.

The general partner's carried interest may be dependent on the IRR. If so, investors should get a third party to verify the IRR calculations.

lead investor The firm or individual that organizes a round of financing and usually contributes the largest amount of capital to the deal.

limited partners (LP) Institutions or individuals that contribute capital to a private equity fund. LPs typically include pension funds, insurance companies, asset management firms, and fund of fund investors.

limited partnership The standard vehicle for investment in private equity funds. A limited partnership has a fixed life, usually of 10 years. The partnership's general partner makes investments, monitors them, and finally exits them for a return on behalf of the investors—limited partners. The GP usually invests the partnership's funds within three to five years, and for the fund's remaining life the GP attempts to achieve the highest possible return for each of the investments by exiting. Occasionally, the limited partnership will have investments that run beyond the fund's life. In this case, partnerships can be extended to ensure that all investments are realized. When all investments are fully divested, a limited partnership can be terminated or wound up.

lock-up period A provision in the underwriting agreement between an investment bank and existing shareholders that prohibits corporate insiders and private equity investors from selling at IPO.

management fee This is the annual fee paid to the general partner. It is typically a percentage of limited partner commitments to the fund and is meant to cover the basic costs of running and administering a fund. Management fees tend to run in the 1.5 percent to 2.5 percent range, and often scale down in the later years of a partnership to reflect the GP's reduced workload. The management fee is not intended to incentivize the investment team—carried interest rewards managers for performance.

portfolio A private equity firm will invest in several companies, each of which is known as a portfolio company. The spread of investments into the various target companies is referred to as the portfolio.

portfolio company This is one of the companies backed by a private equity firm.

placement agent Placement agents are specialists in marketing and promoting private equity funds to institutional investors. They typically charge 2 percent of any capital they help to raise for the fund.

preferred return This is the minimum amount of return that is distributed to the limited partners until the time when the general partner is eligible to deduct carried interest. The preferred return ensures that the general partner shares in the profits of the partnership only after investments have performed well.

private placement When securities are sold without a public offering, this is referred to as a private placement. Generally, this means that the stock is placed with a select number of private investors.

recapitalization This refers to a change in the way a company is financed. It is the result of an injection of capital, either through raising debt or equity.

secondaries The term for the market for interests in venture capital and private equity limited partnerships from the original investors, who are seeking liquidity of their investment before the limited partnership terminates. An original investor might want to sell its stake in a private equity firm for a variety of reasons: it needs liquidity, it has changed investment strategy or focus, or it needs to rebalance its portfolio. The main advantage for investors looking at secondaries is that they can invest in private equity funds over a shorter period than they could with primaries.

secondary buy-out A common exit strategy. This type of buy-out happens when an investment firm's holding in a private company is sold to another investor. For example, one venture capital firm might sell its stake in a private company to another venture capital firm.

secondary market The market for secondary buy-outs. This term should not be confused with secondaries.

second-stage funding The provision of capital to a company that has entered the production and growth stage although it may not be making a profit yet. It is often at this stage that venture capitalists become involved in the financing.

seed capital The provision of very early stage finance to a company with a business venture or idea that has not yet been established. Capital is often provided before venture capitalists become involved. However, a small number of venture capitalists do provide seed capital.

syndication The sharing of deals between two or more investors, normally with one firm serving as the lead investor. Investing together allows venture capitalists to pool resources and share the risk of an investment.

term sheet A summary sheet detailing the terms and conditions of an investment opportunity.

tombstone When a private equity firm has raised a fund, or it wishes to announce a significant closing, it may choose to advertise the event in the financial press—the ad is known as a tombstone. It normally provides details of how much has been raised, the date of closing, and the lead investors.

venture capital The term given to early-stage investments. There is often confusion surrounding this term. Many people use the term *venture capital* very loosely and what they actually mean is private equity.

vintage year The year in which a private equity fund makes its first investment.

Due Diligence Questionnaire

Every investor approaches due diligence differently. Some angel investors may request information in a detailed manner all at once, while others may simply request information at different times or stages. Regardless of an investor's method to obtain information on a potential company, it is a proven fact that exercising thorough due diligence is indicative of more profitable returns. The following documents may be requested in due diligence: www.go4funding.com /Articles/Angel-Investors/Due-Diligence-Checklist.aspx; www.entrepreneur.com/formnet/form/774.

Model Legal Documents

The National Venture Capital Association (NVCA) has put together a set of model venture capital financing documents. This template set of model legal documents for venture capital investments was put together by a group of leading venture capital attorneys, but is offered for your education and familiarization. You are still urged to seek competent, experienced, and professional legal counsel when entering into any financial arrangement. The model venture capital financing documents consist of:

Term Sheet

Stock Purchase Agreement

Certificate of Incorporation

Investor Rights Agreement

Voting Agreement

Right of First Refusal and Co-Sale Agreement

Management Rights Letter

Indemnification Agreement

Model Legal Opinion

They are available for download at www.nvca.org/index
.php?option=com_content&view=article&id=108&Ite
mid=136.

Notes

~

Chapter One: An Historic Overview of Venture Capitalism

1. John F. Kennedy, State of the Union Address, January 30, 1961.

2. Ron Chernow, *Titan: The life of John D. Rockefeller, Sr.* (New York: Random House, 1998), 44–132.

3. Bessemer Venture Partners website, www.bvp.com/about/history.

4. Robert J. Serling, *From the Captain to the Colonel: An Informal History of Eastern Airlines* (New York: Dial Press, 1980).

5. J.H. Whitney & Co. website, "Firm Overview," www.whitney.com /firm-overview.html.

6. Life Sciences Foundation, "The Origins of Venture Capital," San Francisco, 2013, www.lifesciencesfoundation.org/stories-item-76.html.

7. Ibid.

8. C. Addison, "An Oral History of Silicon Valley: Interview with Jay T. Last," Semiconductor Equipment and Materials International, 2007. Copyright 2012. All rights reserved. www.semi.org/en/About /P042813.

9. Joel N. Shurkin, *Broken Genius: The Rise and Fall of William Shockley, Creator of the Electronic Age* (New York: Palgrave Macmillan, 2007).

10. Ibid.; Addison, "An Oral History."

11. Jeff Dorsch, "Synopsys Plans to Purchase Arkos Design for $9.3M," *Electronic News* 41, no. 2071 (June 26, 1995): 8.

12. Michael Riordan, "The Silicon Dioxide Solution: How Physicist Jean Hoerni Built the Bridge from the Transistor to the Integrated Circuit," IEEE Spectrum Online, December 1, 2007, http://spectrum.ieee.org/semiconductors/design/the-silicon-dioxide-solution.

13. Ibid.; Addison, "An Oral History."

14. Rensselaer Polytechnic Institute website, "Alumni Hall of Fame," C. Sheldon Roberts, Class of 1948, www.rpi.edu/about/alumni/inductees/roberts.html.

15. Gordon E. Moore, "The Role of Fairchild in Silicon Technology in the Early Days of 'Silicon Valley,'" *Proceedings of the IEEE* 86, no. 1 (January 1998): 53–62.

16. Ibid.

Chapter Two: The VC Industry Today

1. Donald T. Valentine, "Early Bay Area Venture Capitalists: Shaping the Economic and Business Landscape," an oral history conducted by Sally Smith Hughes in 2009. Regional Oral History Office, The Bancroft Library, University of California, Berkeley, 2010, 59–60.

2. S. Blank, "Why the Lean Start-Up Changes Everything," *Harvard Business Review*, May 2013.

3. Andrew Pollack, "Venture Capital Loses Its Vigor," *New York Times*, October 8, 1989.

4. PricewaterhouseCoopers, "MoneyTree™ Report: Historical Trend Data," May 28, 2013.

5. http://aonetwork.com/aboutao/.

6. http://aonetwork.com/announcing-the-top-10-vc-firms-of-2012/.

7. "The Goliaths: The Fate of Large Firms Helps Explain Economic Volatility," *The Economist*, June 22, 2013.

8. D. Mulcahy, B. Weeks, and H. Bradley, *We Have Met The Enemy . . . And He Is Us: Lessons from Twenty Years of the Kauffman Foundation's Investments in Venture Capital Funds and the Triumph of Hope over Experience* (Kansas City, MO: Ewing Marion Kauffman Foundation, 2012), 2.

9. Ibid., 6.

10. D. Gage, "The Venture Capital Secret: 3 Out of 4 Start-Ups Fail," *Wall Street Journal*, September 19, 2012.

Chapter Three: The Value Proposition

1. "Mend the Money Machine," *The Economist*, May 4, 2013.

2. National Venture Capital Association, "Frequently Asked Questions about Venture Capital," www.nvca.org/.

3. "Venture Impact: The Economic Importance of Venture Backed Companies to the U.S. Economy," a joint study by the National Venture Capital Association and IHS Global Insight, 2011.

4. N. Mitchell, "The Importance of Intellectual Property in Life Science Ventures and How It Impacts Capital Raising," Young Venture Capital Association, June 2, 2006.

5. M. Platzer, "Patient Capital: How Venture Capital Investment Drives Revolutionary Medical Innovation," Content First, LLC, NVCA Medical Industry Group July 24, 2007, 2, 3.

6. R. Grant, "Signia Venture Partners Forming $100M Fund for Mobile, Gaming, Ed-Tech Startups," *GamesBeat*, a subsidiary of *VentureBeat* digital magazine, June 4, 2013, http://venturebeat.com/2013/06/04/signia-venture-partners-forming-100m-fund-for-mobile-gaming-ed-tech-startups/.

7. "3D Printing: A New Brick in the Great Wall," *The Economist*, April 27, 2013.

8. "Orbital in Orbit: Competition Comes to the Celestial Trucking Business," *The Economist*, April 27 2013.

9. "The Twitter Crash: #newscrashrecover—A Hacked Tweet Briefly Unnerves the Stock Market," *The Economist*, April 27, 2013.

10. D. Hornig, "Will Google Glass Change the World?" Casey Daily Dispatch: The Technology Advisor, April 25, 2013, www .caseyresearch.com/cdd/will-google-glass-change-world.

11. "Clean, Safe and It Drives Itself," *The Economist*, April 20, 2013.

12. J. Maudlin, "Thoughts from the Frontline: The Cashless Society," *Mauldin Economics Newsletter*, April 29, 2013, www .mauldineconomics.com/editorial/thoughts-from-the-frontline-the-cashless-society.

13. C. Perry, "In New Mass-Production Technique, Robotic Insects Spring to Life," Wyss Institute for Biologically Inspired Engineering, Harvard School of Engineering and Applied Sciences, Cambridge, Massachusetts, February 15, 2012.

Chapter Four: Prevailing Investment Climate

1. J. Lerner, A. Leamon, and F. Hardymon, *Venture Capital, Private Equity, and the Financing of Entrepreneurship: The Power of Active Investing* (Hoboken, NJ: John Wiley & Sons, 2012), 306.

2. J. Maudlin, "Can It Get Any Better Than This?" *Frontline Newsletter*, August 3, 2013.

3. C. Cox and B. Archer, "Why $16 Trillion Only Hints at the True U.S. Debt," *Wall Street Journal*, November 28, 2012.

4. Federal Reserve Economic Data (FRED), "Federal Debt: Total Public Debt as Percent of Gross Domestic Product," Federal Reserve Bank of St. Louis, August 2, 2013, http://research.stlouisfed.org/fred2/series/GFDEGDQ188S.

5. K. Hall and R. Rankin, "What Should We Do about the National Debt and When?" McClatchy Newspapers, August 17, 2010,

www.mcclatchydc.com/2010/08/17/99285/what-should-we-do
-about-national.html#.Uf_l_JvD_bg#storylink=cpy.

6. Vermont and Indiana do not currently have balanced budget
requirements in their state constitutions.

7. The Committee for a Responsible Federal Budget and Fix the
Debt Coalition, "Summary of the New Simpson-Bowles Plan," blog
post, April 23, 2013, www.fixthedebt.org/blog/summarizing-the-new
-simpson bowles-plan_1#.UgAOoZvD_bh.

8. Joel Palley, "Impact of the Staggers Rail Act of 1980," Office of
Policy: Office of Rail Policy and Development, Federal Railroad
Administration, March 2011.

9. H. Nothhaft and D. Kline, *Great Again: Revitalizing America's
Entrepreneurial Leadership* (Boston: Harvard Business Review Press,
2011).

10. J. Corsi, "Here's the Real Unemployment Rate," WND: Money
(August 2013).

11. "Entrepreneurship and the U.S. Economy," Business Employment
Dynamics, Bureau of Labor Statistics, United States Department of
Labor, 2013, www.bls.gov/bdm/entrepreneurship/entrepreneurship.htm.

Chapter Five: Field Guide for VC Investing Options: Nonlisted

1. M. Ramsinghani, *The Business of Venture Capital: Insights from
Leading Practitioners on the Art of Raising a Fund, Deal Structuring,
Value Creation and Exit Strategies.* (Hoboken, NJ: John Wiley & Sons,
2011), 8.

2. P. Barrett, "Mitt Romney's Box of Kryptonite," *BusinessWeek*, February
23, 2013.

3. J. Ruhnka and J. Young, *A Venture Capital Model of the Development
Process for New Ventures* (New York: Elsevier Science Publishers,
1987).

4. W. Kerr, J. Lerner, and A. Schoar, "The Consequences of Entrepreneurial Finance: A Regression Discontinuity Analysis," National Bureau of Economic Research, NBER Working Paper No. 15831, Cambridge, Massachusetts, March 2010.

5. B. Feld and J. Mendelson, *Venture Deals: Be Smarter than Your Lawyer and Venture Capitalist* (Hoboken, NJ: John Wiley & Sons, 2013).

6. A. Williams, "Collegefeed Raises $1.8M from Accel Partners for Data-Driven Platform That Connects Students and Employers," *TechCrunch* online magazine, August 20, 2013, http://techcrunch.com/2013/08/20/.

7. Benchmark Capital company profile, CrunchBase, August 2013, www.crunchbase.com/financial-organization/benchmark.

8. Ramsinghani, *The Business of Venture Capital*, 157.

9. Sarah Perez, "AngelSoft Relaunches as Gust.com, Now Connects Startups to Investors," *TechCrunch* online magazine, September 13, 2011,http://techcrunch.com/2011/09/13/angelsoft-relaunches-as-gust-com-now-connects-startups-to-investors/.

10. A. Metrick and A. Yasuda, *Venture Capital and the Finance of Innovation*, 2nd ed. (Hoboken, NJ: John Wiley & Sons, 2011), 345–356.

11. J. Lerner, A. Leamon, and F. Hardymon, *Venture Capital, Private Equity, and the Financing of Entrepreneurship: The Power of Active Investing* (Hoboken, NJ: John Wiley & Sons, 2012), 29–30.

12. Ramsinghani, *The Business of Venture Capital*, 20–22.

Chpater Six: Investment Options—Listed

1. A. Pinedo and J. Tanenbaum, "Frequently Asked Questions about PIPEs," Morrison & Foerster LLP, 2013, www.mofo.com/files/Uploads/Images/FAQsPIPEs.pdf.

2. "Speak Softly and Carry a Big PIPE," Ellenoff Grossman & Schole blog, December 2, 2008, http://blog.egsllp.com/2008/12/02/speak-softly-and-carry-a-big-pipe/.

3. N. George, ed., "You Can Bank Better than Buffett," MoneyShow. com blog, August 31, 2011, www.moneyshow.com/investing/article /1/GURU-24338/You-Can-Bank-Better-Than-Buffett/?aid=guru -24338&page=1.

4. D. Miller, "What Is Corporate Venture Capital Funding?" *Access to Capital* newsletter, June 28, 2012, http://accesstocapital.com /corporate-venture-capital-funding/.

5. E. Lee, "News Corp Spinoff Forces Publishing Arm to Prove Growth," Bloomberg.com, June 28, 2013, www.bloomberg.com/news/2013-06 -27/news-corp-spinoff-forces-publishing-arm-to-prove-growth.html.

6. K. Matsa, "Gibbs Takes Over a Troubled *Time* Magazine," FactTank, September 24, 2013,www.pewresearch.org/fact-tank/2013/09/24/ gibbs-takes-over-a-troubled-time-magazine/.

7. Wikipedia, http://en. wikipedia.org/wiki/Publicly_traded_private_ equity.

Chapter Seven: Investment Process— Sourcing and Screening

1. M. Ramsinghani, *The Business of Venture Capital: Insights from Leading Practitioners on the Art of Raising a Fund, Deal Structuring, Value Creation, and Exit Strategies* (Hoboken, NJ: John Wiley & Sons, 2011), 29.

2. B. Feld and J. Mendelson, *Venture Deals: Be Smarter than Your Lawyer and Venture Capitalist*, 2nd ed. (Hoboken, NJ: John Wiley & Sons, 2013), 20.

3. Ramsinghani, *The Business of Venture Capital*, 51.

4. G. Kawasaki, *Reality Check: The Irreverent Guide to Outsmarting, Outmanaging, and Outmarketing Your Competition* (New York: Portfolio, Penguin Group, 2008), 8–29.

5. K. Auletta, *Googled: The End of the World as We Know It* (New York: Penguin Books, 2010), 43.

6. www.forbes.com/profile/kavitark-ram-shriram.

Chapter Eight: Investment Process—Due Diligence and Selection

1. A. Metrick and A. Yasuda, *Venture Capital and the Finance of Innovation*, 2nd ed. (Hoboken, NJ: John Wiley & Sons, 2011), 27–29.

2. L. Kochard, *Foundation and Endowment Investing: Philosophies and Strategies of Top Investors and Institutions* (Hoboken, NJ: John Wiley & Sons, 2008), 169.

3. M. Ramsinghani, *The Business of Venture Capital: Insights from Leading Practitioners on the Art of Raising a Fund, Deal Structuring, Value Creation, and Exit Strategies* (Hoboken, NJ: John Wiley & Sons, 2011), 36.

4. Ramsinghani, *The Business of Venture Capital*, 88.

5. R. Pearce and S. Barnes, *Raising Venture Capital* (Hoboken, NJ: John Wiley & Sons, 2006), 19–23.

6. Institutional Limited Partners Association, "Private Equity Principals," 2011, http://ilpa.org/ilpa-private-equity-principles/.

7. J. Lerner, A. Leamon, and F. Hardymon, *Venture Capital, Private Equity, and the Financing of Entrepreneurship: The Power of Active Investing* (Hoboken, NJ: John Wiley & Sons, 2012), 63–65.

8. S. Blank, "Why the Lean Start-Up Changes Everything," *Harvard Business Review*, May 2013.

9. D. Gage, "The Venture Capital Secret: 3 Out of 4 Start-Ups Fail," *Wall Street Journal*, September 20, 2012.

10. Investopedia, www.investopedia.com/terms/d/duediligence.asp.

11. E. Ries, *The Lean Startup* (New York: Random House, 2011), 81.

12. B. Feld and J. Mendelson, *Venture Deals: Be Smarter than Your Lawyer and Venture Capitalist*, 2nd ed. (Hoboken, NJ: John Wiley & Sons, 2013), 21.

13. A. Osterwalder and Y. Pigneur, *Business Model Generation: A Handbook for Visionaries, Game Changers, and Challengers* (Hoboken, NJ: John Wiley & Sons, 2010).

14. Ramsinghani, *The Business of Venture Capital*, 192–206.

Chapter Nine: Investment Process—Portfolio Construction, Monitoring, and Monetizing

1. National Association of Corporate Directors (NACD), White Paper: "Bridging Effectiveness Gaps: A Candid Look at Board Practices," Washington, DC, 2013, 7. Reprinted with the permission of the National Association of Corporate Directors.

2. The Working Group on Director Accountability and Board Effectiveness, *A Simple Guide to the Basic Responsibilities of VC-Backed Company Directors* (San Francisco: Levensohn Venture Partners LLC, 2007), 1.

3. M. Ramsinghani, *The Business of Venture Capital: Insights from Leading Practitioners on the Art of Raising A Fund, Deal Structuring, Value Creation, and Exit Strategies* (Hoboken, NJ: John Wiley & Sons, 2011), 256–261.

4. E. Paley, "How Not to Get Fired," *Inc. Magazine*, July/August 2013, 36.

5. J. Lerner, A. Leamon, and F. Hardymon, *Venture Capital, Private Equity, and the Financing of Entrepreneurship: The Power of Active Investing* (Hoboken, NJ: John Wiley & Sons, 2012), 198–201.

6. Ernst & Young, "Globalizing Venture Capital: Global Venture Capital Insights and Trends Report 2011," New York, 17.

7. Ramsinghani, *The Business of Venture Capital*, 299–310.

8. J. Ritter, X. Gao, and Z. Zhu, "Where Have All the IPOs Gone?" Chicago: Social Science Research Network, University of Chicago, Booth School of Business, August 26, 2013, http://ssrn.com/abstract =1954788.

9. Ramsinghani, *The Business of Venture Capital*, 321–322.

10. D. Ibrahim, "The New Exit in Venture Capital," *Vanderbilt University Law Review* 65, no. 1 (January 2012): 7.

About the Authors

LOUIS C. GERKEN founded San Francisco Bay Area-based Gerken Capital Associates (GCA) in 1989. GCA is an independent, alternative asset fund manager and advisor. Prior to forming GCA, Mr. Gerken was Managing Director and Group Head of Prudential Securities' Technology Investment Banking Division, and earlier a General Partner with Prudential Securities' Prutech Venture Capital Funds. As one of the largest U.S. venture capital funds, Prutech was responsible for completing over 50 IT and biotech sector early- and expansion-stage investments, and was one of the first VC funds to pioneer corporate partnering as a co-investment strategy. Prior, Mr. Gerken oversaw VC activities for Wells Fargo Bank, where he launched one of the very first U.S. fund of funds. Mr. Gerken is a father of one and resides in the Bay Area.

WESLEY A. WHITTAKER has been writing professionally for more than 35 years. He has worked steadily as a ghostwriter and editor in the business and finance sector since penning the critically acclaimed John Wiley & Sons offering, *Economic Warfare: Secrets of Wealth Creation in the Age of Welfare Politics*, for Ziad Abdelnour in 2011. This is his third nonfiction book and second book for Wiley. He holds a BA in Management and Organizational Development from Spring Arbor University.